W9-BAS-030

Aran Sweater Design

Aran Sweater Design

by Janet Szabo

Big Sky Knitting Designs

Photographs and drawings: Big Sky Knitting Designs
Cover photography by Karen Weyer Photography, Kalispell, MT
Cover design by Teresa Sales

The charts in this book were created with Knitters Symbol Fonts,
copyrighted material made available
as shareware by Golden Fleece Publications.

© 2006 Janet Szabo
All Rights Reserved

Second Printing 2007

Big Sky Knitting Designs
3720 Foothill Road
Kalispell, MT 59901

Printed in the United States of America

ISBN 0-9768025-0-3

reface

My doctor often tells me that she wishes she could have my life. I find that extraordinarily amusing, because I came very close to having *her* life. I declined a place in medical school many years ago because at the last minute I had a gut feeling that it wasn't what I was supposed to be doing. And my poor husband, victim of a bait-and-switch scam, now finds himself married to a professional knitter, not a doctor. I don't believe he has ever complained, although I think he's a bit bewildered by it all.

I became a professional knitter by accident. (I didn't become a knitter by accident— that was a very deliberate gift from my mother.) I might have continued happily as a recreational knitter were it not for the fact that we moved to Montana where jobs paying a living wage are far from plentiful. Imagine that you are offered a position with a software company and the interviewer informs you that the company "is prepared to pay you a bit more than minimum wage because you are so qualified"! Please.

My self-employed-as-a-builder husband suggested that instead of turning the family upside-down to bring home $300 a month, I stay home and figure out some way to make money from my knitting. I love a challenge, and he knows that. I should add that shortly after that, I was diagnosed with acute myelogenous leukemia and spent six months in the hospital undergoing chemotherapy. (Did I say I love a challenge?) I tell you, there is nothing like staring your own mortality in the face to motivate you to stop wasting time and figure out how to make money from your knitting.

Two books and a newsletter later I continue to be grateful that I passed on medical school. I've managed to craft a career that has allowed me to be involved in the lives of my kids, my husband, and my community while finding professional fulfillment doing something I love. On any given day I might be a teacher, a writer, a publisher, or—my favorite job of all—a knitter. All of it might have happened by accident, but I can't imagine wanting my life to be any other way.

cknowledgements

Projects of this size and scope aren't possible without the help of several key people. I would not want to attempt a publishing project without the assistance of my technical editor, JC Briar. JC has kept me on the straight and narrow for several years now as the technical editor of my newsletter, *Twists and Turns: The Newsletter for Lovers of Cable Knitting*. Her eagle eye and practical advice have elevated my work to a level far beyond what I could accomplish on my own.

One of the side effects of writing about knitting is that it leaves less and less time for the actual knitting. Donna Walker has also been involved with *Twists and Turns*—and now this book—as my test-knitter. She works through the first drafts of my knitting patterns with speed and good humor, transforming a nebulous design idea into a finished product. Intially I felt rather like a bad mother, farming my children out to someone else to raise, but Donna has been a good foster mom to my designs.

My husband and two girls also deserve a word of thanks, and apologies for all those nights they had to eat frozen pizzas. I hope my girls have learned that creativity comes in many forms, including the kind that allowed their mother to write a book while managing to go on field trips, help with the school band, and chauffeur them to piano and ballet lessons—essentially being in multiple places at the same time. I know that sometimes the strain of all that multi-tasking made me short-temperered but I also think that they know now that being a mom does not mean losing yourself as an intelligent, talented person.

And after all this time, my husband and I have finally reached an agreement. I don't look at his garage full of tools and he doesn't look at my basement full of yarn.

How to Use This Book

Organizing this book was rather like trying to compartmentalize a plate of spaghetti: all the parts are interconnected. Nevertheless, I managed to impose a bit of linear structure on the process of designing and knitting an Aran sweater.

This book is divided into three parts. Part One—Chapters 1 through 7—provides the background and design fundamentals needed to create a design. By studying these chapters, you'll begin to see what elements are common to Aran sweaters and how those elements can be combined in aesthetically pleasing ways.

Part Two—Chapters 8 through 15—presents the nuts-and-bolts details required to take a design from concept to completion. Whether your design is simple or complex, casual or tailored, the information in these chapters will help you make the journey from a sketch or a swatch to a finished garment. Please note, however, that the design information presented is that which is unique to Aran sweaters. For more general design information, I suggest you consult one of the books listed in Appendix A.

Part Three—Chapters 16 through 19—provides concrete examples of several different Aran garment styles. Use them as a road map of sorts—study the planning behind them and use them as inspiration for your own unique designs.

Table of Contents

Preface   v

Acknowledgements   vi

How to Use This Book   vii

Part One—Aran Background and Fundamentals   1

1 A Brief History   3

2 Anatomy of an Aran   5

3 Materials   7

    3.1 Yarn Construction   7

        3.1.1 Woolen- vs. Worsted-Spun Yarns   7

        3.1.2 Plies and Stitch Definition   8

    3.2 Yarn Quantity   9

    3.3 Yarn Colors   9

    3.4 Needles   10

    3.5 Stitch Dictionaries   10

    3.6 Graph Paper   10

    3.7 Computer-Aided Design   10

4 Learning the Ropes (and Honeycombs and Diamonds. . .)   13

    4.1 Cable Nomenclature   13

    4.2 Cable Charts   15

    4.3 Cable Knitting Basics   16

        4.3.1 Ropes   16

        4.3.2 Waves   17

        4.3.3 Double Cables   18

        4.3.4 Plaits and Braids   19

        4.3.5 Zig-Zags   20

        4.3.6 Diamonds and Triangles   21

        4.3.7 Lace and Cables   23

        4.3.8 Slip-Stitch Cables   24

        4.3.9 Closed-Ring Designs 25

        4.3.10 Ribbed Cables   26

4.3.11 Oddball Cables   27

4.3.12 Smocked Cables   29

4.3.13 Embellished Cables   30

4.3.14 Intarsia and Multi-Colored Cables   31

4.4 Other Aran Design Elements   33

4.4.1 Twisted Stitches and Stitches That Twist   33

4.4.2 Trims   35

4.4.3 Filler Stitches   36

4.4.4 Knots, Bobbles, and Popcorn Stitches   37

5 Creating a Design   39

5.1 Planning the Cable Layout   40

5.1.1 Body Measurements   40

5.1.2 Design Balance   40

5.1.2.1 A Bit of Math   41

5.1.2.2 Scale   42

5.1.2.3 Sibling Rivalry—or Why Some Patterns Get Along and Some Don't   42

5.1.2.4 The Layout   44

5.1.2.5 Row Repeats   46

                                                                   47

5.1.3 Cable Splay   50

5.1.4 Vertical Placement   51

5.1.5 Cable Orientation   52

5.2 Creative Options   53

5.3 Using "Unique" Cable Patterns   54

6 Putting It All Together   57

6.1 Swatching   57

6.2 Choosing a Garment Style   58

6.3 Coordinating the Garment   59

6.3.1 The Body   59

6.3.2 The Trim   60

6.3.3 The Sleeves   60

6.3.3.1 Dropped-Shoulder and Peasant Sleeves   61

6.3.3.2 Set-in Sleeves   61

6.3.4 The Saddles   63

6.3.4.1 Perpendicular Join   64

6.3.4.2 Sewing In   65

6.3.4.3 Picking Up Along Saddle Edges and Knitting Down   65

7 Useful Aran Knitting Tips   67

7.1 Moving Stitches   67

7.1.1 Cable Needles   67

7.1.2 Cabling Without a Needle   67

7.2 Marking the Work   68

7.2.1 Stitch Markers   68

7.2.2 Row Markers   69

7.2.3 Hang Tags   69

7.3 Better Bobbles   69

7.3.1 Tip #1: Use Yarn Overs   69

7.3.2 Tip #2: Pair the Decreases   69

7.3.3 Tip #3: Strangle the Bobble   70

7.3.4 Tip #4: Learn to Knit Back Backwards   70

7.4 Decreasing Into Cables   70

7.5 Easier Finishing   71

7.5.1 Filler Stitches   71

7.5.2 Armhole Edges   71

7.6 Fixing Mistakes   71

7.7 Tubular Cast-On For Neckband   73

Part Two—From Concept to Sweater   75

8 Constructing an Aran   77

8.1 Bottom-Up Construction   77

8.1.1 Knitting Bottom-up Flat Pieces   77

8.1.2 Knitting Bottom-up in the Round   78

8.2 Top-Down Construction   79

8.2.1 Neckband-First   80

8.2.2 Body First   83

    8.2.2.1 Top-Down Arans With Saddles   83

    8.2.2.2 Top-Down Arans Without Saddles   86

9 Dropped-Shoulder Arans   89

  9.1 Dropped-Shoulder Arans With Saddles   90

    9.1.1 Knitting Bottom-up Flat Pieces   90

    9.1.2 Knitting Bottom-Up in the Round   91

    9.1.3 Knitting From the Top   92

  9.2 Dropped-Shoulder Arans Without Saddles   94

    9.2.1 Knitting Bottom-up Flat Pieces   94

    9.2.2 Knitting Bottom-up in the Round   94

    9.2.3 Knitting From the Top   95

10 Peasant Sleeve Arans   97

  10.1 Peasant-Sleeve Arans With Saddles   98

    10.1.1 Knitting Bottom-up Flat Pieces   98

    10.1.2 Knitting Bottom-up in the Round   99

    10.1.3 Knitting From the Top   100

  10.2 Peasant-Sleeve Arans Without Saddles   103

    10.2.1 Knitting Bottom-up Flat Pieces   103

    10.2.2 Knitting Bottom-up in the Round   104

    10.2.3 Knitting From the Top   104

11 Set-In Sleeve Arans   107

  11.1 Set-In Sleeve Arans With Saddles   109

    11.1.1 Knitting Bottom-up Flat Pieces   109

    11.1.2 Knitting From the Top   110

  11.2 Set-In Sleeve Arans Without Saddles   115

    11.2.1 Knitting Bottom-up Flat Pieces   115

    11.2.2 Knitting From the Top   115

12 Raglan Sleeve Arans   119

  12.1 Knitting Bottom-up in the Round   119

  12.2 Knitting From the Top   120

13 Aran Vests   123
   13.1 Aran Vests—With or Without Saddles   124
14 T-Sleeve Arans   127
   14.1 T-Sleeve Aran Construction   127
15 Wide-Saddle Arans   131
   15.1 Wide-Saddle Version #1   131
   15.2 Wide-Saddle Version #2   132

Part Three—Aran Sweater Projects   137
16 Aran Vest Project   139
17 Aran Pullover Project   145
18 Set-In Sleeve Aran Project   151
19 Raglan Aran Cardigan Project   157

Appendix A—Resources   165
Appendix B—Measurements Worksheet   168
Appendix C—Key to Charts   170
Index   173

Part One

Aran Background and Fundamentals

 Brief History

Many popular sweater styles such as the Fair Isle and Scottish fisher gansey have their roots in hundreds of years of ethnic tradition. For years, the story circulated around the knitting community that the Aran style came from just such a long and honored tradition. It was obvious, claimed its promoters, that the sculpted, flowing, three-dimensional quality of the stitch patterns was based on the ancient Celtic artwork found throughout that region. Women of the Aran islands knitted these magical motifs into the garments worn by their fishermen husbands and sons, and should they happen to meet an unfortunate end in the sea, the characteristic patterns could be used to identify them when their bodies washed up on shore. It made enough sense that no one really questioned the truth of the story.

The knitting world owes a debt of gratitude to Alice Starmore for her painstaking research into the true origins of the Aran sweater style. By examining the earliest surviving examples of Aran knitting, she was able to document the evolution of the Aran style in the early years of the 20th century from the Scottish fisher gansey into the garment we are familiar with today. Starmore maintains that it was a single "skilled and imaginative knitter" who took the components of the Scottish fisher gansey and metamorphosed them into the cabled, heavily textured style of garment we know as an Aran. I highly recommend her book, *Aran Knitting*, for the historical information it provides as well as for her inspiring designs.

Voltaire said, "History consists of a series of accumulated imaginative inventions." Brief though it may be, I believe we can argue that the history of the Aran sweater is, and continues to be, made up of those wonderful accumulated imaginative inventions. May we, as knitters, add richly to that history.

Anatomy of an Aran

A knitting tradition doesn't have to have a long history for it to be a legitimate and recognizable style. Identify a garment as an "Irish fisherman knit" or "Aran sweater" and many people will have an accurate mental image. Figure 1, below, shows a number of elements common to Aran sweaters.

Debate continues, though, about what constitutes a "traditional" Aran sweater—is it the presence or absence of saddle shoulders? Is it the arrangement of the cable patterns? Is it the use of a specific kind of yarn?

In *Aran Knitting*, Alice Starmore defines the traditional Aran as "a hand knitted garment of flat construction, composed of vertical panels of cabled geometric patterns and textured stitches. On each piece of the sweater there is a central panel, flanked by symmetrically arranged side panels. The use of heavy, undyed cream wool is a classic— though not essential—component of the style."

This definition provides a good starting point for those knitters who want to design their own Arans. But just as the "skilled and imaginative knitter" who invented the Aran sweater was not bound by the traditional method of knitting Scottish fisher ganseys, today's knitters should not feel it necessary to stick to the traditional methods of flat construction and symmetrical pattern layout in order to design an aesthetically pleasing garment. The essential elements of a traditional Aran sweater lend themselves well to experimentation. Will the resulting design be a traditional Aran in the truest historical sense of the style? Perhaps not. However, it *will*

Saddle shoulders

Wide center cable panel

Filler stitch

Narrow side cable panels

Fig. 1: *Common elements of Aran sweaters.*

be a unique and interesting garment.

Aran sweater design can be challenging, certainly, but it is not beyond the reach of those who are willing to learn the fundamental concepts. The aim of this book is to give you the confidence to design an Aran sweater that shows off your unique, creative knitting talents.

Materials

Designing and knitting an Aran sweater does not require an arsenal of sophisticated tools; remember that the knitters of the very first Arans had only yarn, needles, and imagination. Modern knitters have those supplies, and more, at their disposal.

3.1 Yarn Construction

The appeal of the Aran sweater lies as much in the yarn used to knit the sweater as in the cable patterning itself. The Scottish fisher gansey which gave rise to the Aran sweater traditionally was knit in a firmly spun 5-ply yarn. Why is that important? In order to answer that, we need to pause for a short discussion about yarn construction.

Unless you are a spinner as well as a knitter, you're probably not aware of the differences in yarns. You might recognize that some yarns aren't suitable for certain projects, but you don't know exactly why. Think about what draws you to a yarn—for example, when you walk in to a yarn store, why do you gravitate to a particular yarn? For most of us, it's the color. We're immediately drawn to a yarn because it's red, or blue, or that elusive shade of chartreuse we've been searching for. Only after we pick up a yarn do we notice that it's soft, or harsh, or smooth, or hairy. Aside from the cable patterns in a design, the construction of the yarn has the biggest impact on the final look of the project.

3.1.1 Woolen- vs. Worsted-Spun Yarns

Yarns can be divided broadly into two categories: woolen-spun and worsted-spun. Note—and this is very important—that "woolen" used in this context refers to the construction of a yarn, not the fiber content. Woolen-spun yarns can be spun from wool, cotton, cashmere, and many other fibers. Note also that "worsted" used in this context refers to the construction of the yarn, not the weight. Worsted-spun yarns can range from fingering weight to bulky weight.

For purposes of this discussion, "woolen-spun" and "worsted-spun" will comprise the two ends of a yarn continuum. In between are many "semi-woolen" and "semi-worsted" yarns—yarns which have characteristics of both woolen-spun and worsted-spun construction. Once you recognize the differences between these yarns, you'll be better able to make educated decisions about what yarn to use for a project.

Woolen-Spun Yarns	Worsted-Spun Yarns
They are spun from shorter fibers, from 1" to 2" in length. Sheep breeds that produce these shorter fibers are Merino, Columbia, Targhee, and Shetland.	They are spun from long fibers, anything from 4" to 11" in length. Sheep breeds that produce these longer fibers include Lincoln, Cotswold, Wensleydale, Bluefaced Leicester, and other "longwool" breeds.
Wool fibers used in woolen-spun yarns tend to be very crimpy or wavy.	The fibers are generally straight or slightly wavy, and may have a shiny surface that reflects light.
The fibers are carded before spinning, which produces a web of randomly-arranged fibers of varying lengths.	The fibers are combed before spinning to remove short fibers and vegetable matter. The fibers which are left are uniform in length and are parallel to one another.
The spinning method preserves the loftiness and elasticity of the fibers; woolen-spun yarns do not have as much twist as worsted-spun yarns, making them feel less harsh against the skin.	The spinning method preserves the fibers' parallel arrangement. Worsted-spun yarns contain a lot of twist.
A woolen-spun yarn is not as durable as a worsted-spun yarn because it has a greater tendency to pill.	The surface of the yarn is smooth, durable, and long-wearing. Worsted yarns are the least likely yarns to pill.
A woolen-spun yarn has better insulating qualities than a worsted-spun yarn.	Because very little air is trapped within the fibers during spinning, worsted yarns are not very insulating.

You may ask, "Which yarn is the better choice for an Aran sweater?" The answer is, "It depends." Much depends upon the result you, the knitter, are looking for. If you want to showcase your knitting talents with complicated cable patterning, a worsted-spun yarn will likely show it off to better advantage. If, however, you want to knit a sweater that will keep you warm on the slopes, a woolen-spun yarn might be a better choice. You will read this advice over and over again in upcoming chapters: swatching is the best way to determine if a particular yarn is suitable for a project.

3.1.2 Plies and Stitch Definition

Another factor in the choice of yarns for an Aran—but one which is less obvious—is the number of plies in a yarn. Note that some knitters (those outside of the U.S. and those who have been knitting for 50 or 60 years) may be more familiar with "ply" as a designation for weight, *e.g.*, a 2-ply is thinner than a 4-ply or an 8-ply. Here, "ply" refers to the number of individual strands making up a multi-ply yarn.

A singles yarn will give adequate stitch definition, but has the unfortunate tendency to "bias" or slant on the diagonal. This is because the process of adding twist to the fibers adds energy to the strand of yarn that is not balanced out by another strand twisting in the opposite direction. The twist energy makes itself apparent in the slant of the fabric. This is not to say that singles yarns are unsuitable, simply that they need to be spun loosely enough so that the bias is less apparent. Beware of singles yarns that are so tightly twisted that they kink up on themselves.

A 2-ply yarn is the favorite of handspinners anxious to complete the spinning process and begin knitting with their yarn. A 2-ply yarn is created by twisting two strands of yarns together in the direction opposite of that in which they were spun. Plying a yarn balances out its twist and makes it less likely to bias. Plying also makes the yarn thicker than the individual plies composing it.

Plying more than two strands of yarn together yields yarns which not only increase in diameter, but have a rounder cross-section, as well (see Figure 2).

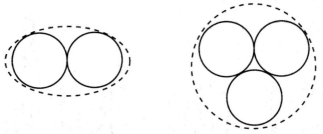

Fig. 2, L to R: *Cross-section of a 2-ply yarn, cross-section of a 3-ply yarn.*

This rounder cross-section provides a subtle improvement in stitch definition. As a spinner and knitter, I concluded that this improvement was enough to justify the extra work it takes to create a 3-, 4-, or 5-ply yarn instead of just a 2-ply yarn.

3.2 Yarn Quantity

Aran sweaters require more yarn than is required for a Stockinette Stitch sweater in the same size. Cables use up more yarn. A women's medium-to-large sweater uses approximately 1800 yards of worsted-weight yarn. A man's large can use as much as 2500 yards. Buy extra. You can always make a matching hat or mittens with the leftovers.

3.3 Yarn Colors

Arans traditionally have been knit in light-colored yarns, because lighter colors show off the patterning to best advantage. However, don't be afraid to experiment with other colors. Jewel toned yarns make lovely Arans. The darker browns, grays and black tend to swallow up the patterning, but can be used successfully with good planning.

Consider adding color to Aran sweaters in the form of embroidery, Fair Isle/cable combinations, or by knitting each cable panel in a different color using intarsia.

3.4 Needles

Needle preferences are very personal, and each knitter needs to find those needles which are most comfortable. For instance, I don't like to use the nickel-plated knitting needles. They are too slippery for me; I find myself clutching the yarn and needles which eventually makes my hands cramp up. I much prefer the coated aluminum needles, but even within that category I have a preference for needles with very sharp tips. Sharp-tipped needles make working complex stitch maneuvers, such as those found in Trinity Stitch, much easier. Some knitters may prefer wood or bamboo. Much depends upon the type of fiber you are using and the way you knit. Experiment until you find those needles which are most comfortable for you to use.

3.5 Stitch Dictionaries

Fortunately, we do not—like knitters of old—have to commit stitch patterns to memory. Stitch dictionaries are essential tools in any Aran designer's collection. Acquire as many as you can, and if you can only afford one or two, by all means, make sure they are one or two of the Barbara Walker *Treasuries*.

You will find that you can also modify existing stitch patterns into completely new ones (indeed, there are professional knitters who specialize in creating new stitch patterns), but when you are just starting out, you will probably want to refer to existing patterns. See Appendix A for a complete list.

3.6 Graph Paper

Graph paper is for laying out patterns and drawing schematics of your design. The larger the sheet of paper, the better. The squares can be any size, but five squares to the inch will allow you to draw schematics to scale. Drafting supply stores are good places to find large tablets of graph paper. Get a ruler and some sharp pencils to go with it.

3.7 Computer-Aided Design

It's not critical, but having access to a computer with charting software can make designing much easier. I often print out several repeats of the charts for the cable patterns in a design, and paste them onto a large piece of paper to get an idea of how they will be placed on the garment. Some basic pattern drafting computer programs are also available to aid in drafting different garment styles.

Learning the Ropes (and Honeycombs and Diamonds...) 4

Cables are the cornerstone of Aran design. Flip through any stitch dictionary and be astounded by the number and variety of cable patterns available to today's knitter. Mix and match these patterns to create an infinite number of interesting designs. Make a design bold and aggressive, elegant and refined, or quiet and delicate, simply through the selection of cables and their placement within the design.

Don't be intimidated by designing with or knitting cables. Cables look complicated, but they are simply stitches crossing over other stitches. The crossings can be composed of knit stitches crossing over knit stitches, knit stitches crossing over purl stitches, or some combination of both. In most cases, the crossing maneuvers are quite logical and easily understood. A stitch or group of stitches is removed from the working needle and placed on a holder. This holder is held at the front of the work to make a cable which crosses to the left, or held at the back of the work to make a cable which crosses to the right. Some of the fancier cable patterns have more intricate crossing maneuvers requiring that more than one group of stitches be held on holders.

Designing with cables—and especially, designing a full-blown Aran—is much easier once the basic concepts of cable formation have been mastered. Seeing how larger cables evolve from smaller ones and why some cable combinations work and some don't becomes second nature. In time, creating new and unique cable patterns might even be something to try. This chapter begins by examining how cables are described in knitting terms, then looking at examples of each type of cable. Examples of "non-cable" components of Aran sweaters, such as filler stitches and ribbings, are also included.

4.1 Cable Nomenclature

As with many other aspects of knitting, there is no single universal method of describing cables in written knitting patterns. Barbara Walker uses one system in her *Treasuries*, the Harmony series of stitch pattern books uses another system, and still other naming systems are used by magazines and in computer software. The following table illustrates just how confusing it can be when the same cable is classified differently by different naming systems:

Cable Maneuver	Walker's *Treasuries*	Harmony Stitch Guides	*Knitter's Magazine*
Slip next stitch to cable needle and hold at back of work, k2, k1 from cable needle	BC: Back Cross	C3B: Cable 3 Back	2/1 RC (2/1 Right Cross)
Slip next 2 sts to cable needle and hold at front of work, p1, k2 from cable needle	FC: Front Cross	T3B: Twist 3 Front	2/1 LPC (2/1 Left Purl Cross)
Slip next 2 sts to cable needle and hold at back of work, k2, k2 from cable needle	BKC: Back Knit Cross	C4B: Cable 4 Back	2/2 RC (2/2 Right Cross)
Slip next 2 sts to cable needle and hold at front of work, p2, k2 from cable needle	FC: Front Cross	T4F: Twist 4 Front	2/2 LPC (2/2 Left Purl Cross)

I don't care for Barbara Walker's cable abbreviations because she uses the same abbreviation (*e.g.*, FC for Front Cross) to describe more than one cable manuever. For example, in *A Second Treasury of Knitting Patterns*, the abbreviation FC in the Telescope Lattice pattern means "slip 2 stitches to cable needle and hold in front, k2, then k2 from cable needle." In the Rib and Braid pattern, FC means "slip 1 stitch to cable needle and hold at front, p1, then k1 from cable needle." Just when you think you have the definition of FC memorized, it changes!

The abbreviations used in the Harmony stitch books are more consistent, but still do not describe adequately the cable crossing maneuvers.

My favorite cable naming system is the one used by *Knitter's Magazine* and by other contemporary knitting publications. It not only indicates which way the cable crosses (R or L), it specifies how many stitches cross over how many stitches, and what stitch maneuvers (knit or purl) are involved. For example:

> 1/1 RC means "slip 1 st to cable needle and hold at back, k1, k1 from cable needle"
> 1/2 LPC means "slip 1 st to cable needle and hold at front, p2, then k1 from cable needle"
> 2/2 RC means "slip 2 sts to cable needle and hold at back, k2, then k2 from cable needle"

3/3 LPC means "slip 3 sts to cable needle and hold at front, p3, then k3 from cable needle"

It's clear that whenever the instructions include an "R" it means that the cable leans to the right and the stitches on the cable needle should be held at the back of the work. If the instructions include an "L" it means that the cable leans to the left and the stitches on the cable needle should be held at the front of the work. If the instructions include a "P" it means that some of the stitches in the crossing should be purled. However, even this much descriptive information does not eliminate the need for a comprehensive list of abbreviations and what they mean; it simply makes it easier to understand the abbreviation within the body of the pattern.

If you're using several cable patterns in a design, and they come from different stitch pattern books using different naming systems, it's best to pick one system and use it for all the cable patterns in your design. That is especially important if you are writing down your instructions for other knitters to follow.

Most cables also have fanciful common names (*e.g.*, Aran Honeycomb, Ladder of Life, *etc.*) which are somewhat descriptive, but do not describe how the cable is knitted. To further muddy the waters, the same cable pattern may be known by different common names, depending upon the source. Unless otherwise noted, when speaking of a cable by its common name, I will use the name given by Barbara Walker in *A Treasury of Knitting Patterns*, *A Second Treasury of Knitting Patterns*, *Charted Knitting Designs*, and *A Fourth Treasury of Knitting Patterns*.

4.2 Cable Charts

I strongly recommend working from charts whenever possible. Some knitters insist that they cannot work from charts and can only work from written instructions. I understand, because I used to be one of those knitters. It takes a bit of practice, but I believe everyone can learn to work from charts. Perhaps the most important reason for working from charts is that a chart gives an immediate visual confirmation of the pattern. Compare the knitted fabric to the chart and see instantly if there is an error. Becoming comfortable with a visual representation of the knitted fabric also leads to less reliance on charts or written instructions—it becomes easier to "read" the knitting and anticipate the next cable crossing.

However, even charted instructions are not perfect. A number of different sets of knitting symbols are currently in use, and all differ slightly. Knitters who draw their charts by hand can use whichever set of symbols they like. (I recommend the set Barbara Walker uses in *Charted Knitting Designs*.) Commercial charting software is available, but the programs and capabilities differ widely.

4.3 Cable Knitting Basics

I could devote an entire book just to cable stitches. Because cables used in Aran designs are a smaller subset of the vast number of cables, I'll confine this discussion to the cables and cabling techniques most likely to be seen and used in an Aran design. The discussion starts with the most basic of cables and progress to the more complicated and esoteric ones. Along the way it will become clear how certain kinds of cables evolve from others, which may inspire you to try designing your own cable patterns for your next Aran.

We'll also explore some of the non-cabled elements—such as bobbles and filler stitches—that are part of Aran design.

4.3.1 Ropes

Ropes are the most basic of cable forms, and it's easy to see how the Aran sweater developed as a result of their use in fisher gansey designs. The most basic cross of one stitch over one stitch, repeated every other row, is a type of rope cable. This cross is always in the same direction—either to the right or to the left.

A "classic" rope cable is one which crosses at row intervals equal to the number of stitches in the cable—*e.g.*, a 4-stitch rope cable crosses every fourth row, a 6-stitch rope cable crosses every sixth row, *etc.* Crossing stitches at smaller intervals produces a tighter cable, and crossing them at greater intervals produces a looser cable.

Figure 3 shows a group of rope cables of varying thicknesses and appearances. From left to right: a two-stitch rope cable crossing every other row; a four-stitch rope cable crossing every fourth row; a six-stitch rope cable crossing every sixth row; a six-stitch rope cable alternately crossing every fourth then tenth row; and a six-stitch rope cable crossing every eighth row with two rows of Reverse Stockinette Stitch worked over the four middle stitches.

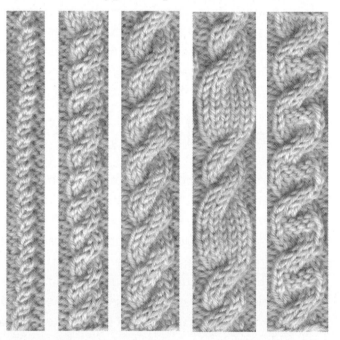

Fig. 3, L to R: *Two-Stitch Rope Cable, Four-Stitch Rope Cable, Six-Stitch Rope Cable, Eccentric Cable, Cross-Banded Cable.*

Because of their strong vertical appearance, rope cables make good dividers between larger cable panels in an Aran design. The two-stitch rope cable is a particularly useful divider between cables.

4.3.2 Waves

Wave cables are like rope cables, but alternately cross to the right and to the left. Because they are not as strongly vertical in appearance as rope cables, they tend to be a bit more subtle when used as dividers in a design. Like rope cables, work them over two, four, six, or even more stitches. Figure 4 shows two wave cables: one worked over two stitches and one worked over four stitches.

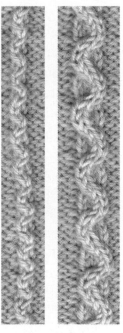

Fig. 4, L to R: *Two-Stitch Wave Cable, Four-Stitch Wave Cable.*

4.3.3 Double Cables

Double cables are simply adjacent rope or wave cables twisting in opposition to each other.

Double rope cables which consistently twist toward or away from each other form shapes resembling horseshoes. As with rope cables, double cables can be made tighter or looser in appearance by increasing or decreasing the frequency of cabling rows. Figure 5 illustrates a variety of these horseshoe shapes. From left to right: a four-stitch horseshoe cable; an eight-stitch horseshoe cable; an eight-stitch cable with alternating left and right crossings; a horseshoe cable in which the component rope cables are formed by crossing one stitch over three stitches and where one additional knit stitch is placed in the middle of the cable.

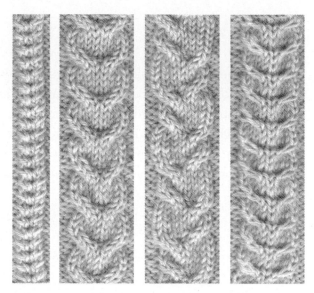

Fig. 5, L to R: *Four-Stitch Horseshoe Cable, Eight-Stitch Horseshoe Cable, Alternating Cable, Claw Cable.*

Figure 6 shows how double wave cables which alternately twist toward, then away from, each other form the classic Aran cable pattern known as Aran Honeycomb. From left to right: two-stitch wave cables forming a small Aran Honeycomb; four-stitch wave cables forming a large Aran Honeycomb. The Aran Honeycomb cable, repeated over a multiple of eight stitches, forms the Aran Honeycomb cable panel, which is the basis of many Aran designs. Working the Aran Honeycomb over 12 stitches (two adjacent six-stitch wave cables) produces an even larger version of this cable pattern which can be filled in with moss, seed, or other filler stitches.

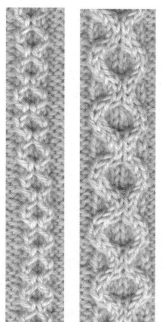

Fig. 6, L to R: *Four-Stitch Aran Honeycomb Cable, Eight-Stitch Aran Honeycomb Cable.*

4.3.4 Plaits and Braids

At first glance, plaits and braids may seem to be the same. However, there is a distinction, though subtle. All plaits are braids, but not all braids are plaits. A plait is composed of three strands; therefore, it needs to be a cable containing a multiple of three stitches (three, six, nine, *etc.*). The strands of a plait cross only over each other—they do not move over any background stitches.

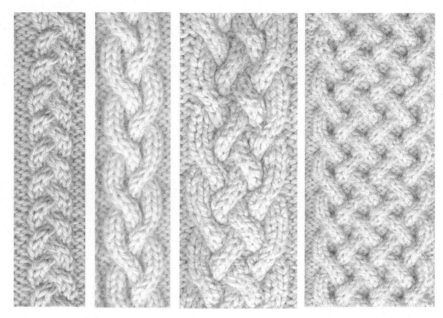

Fig. 7, L to R: *Six-Stitch Plait, a three-strand braid, Five-Fold Aran Braid, a braid panel.*

A braid, in contrast, can be composed of any number of strands containing any number of stitches. The strands of a braid move over each other like the strands of a plait, but unlike plaits, they may also move back and forth over background stitches. The movement of braid strands over background stitches opens up the appearance of the braid and makes it less dense than a plait.

Plaits and braids are wonderfully versatile elements of Aran design. Narrow plaits make good dividers between larger cables, while thicker plaits are bold and dramatic. Braids can be used not only as individual cables, but also as center panels when worked over a large multiple of stitches. Varying the number of background stitches between the strands of a braid makes it denser or looser in appearance. The strands of a braid can also move irregularly across the background stitches to form many other types of geometric shapes. Some cable patterns which look nothing like traditional braids often have braided sections within them.

Figure 7 shows a variety of plaits and braids. From left to right: a plait composed of three two-stitch strands; a three-strand braid with a single purl stitch between the strands; a five-strand braid, also with a single purl stitch between the strands; a braid panel, with two purl stitches between each strand.

4.3.5 Zig-Zags

Columns of knit stitches moving back and forth across a background of purl stitches form an assortment of zig-zagging lines.

Depending upon the number of stitches involved in the cross, the lines can undulate softly across the fabric, or swerve sharply back and forth. Lines can be single or paired, and paired lines can move in parallel or can cross over and under each other. Because of their swinging, angular appearance, these cables are best framed by straight cable shapes (such as braids or ropes) to keep them from "bumping into" other cables in the design. Also, it's aesthetically pleasing to work mirror images of these cables on either side of the center panel.

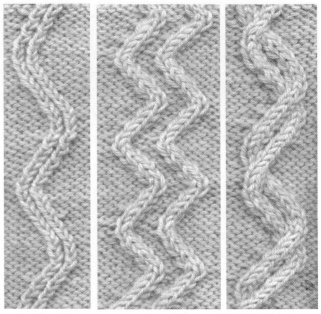

Fig. 8, L to R: *Two adjacent-stitch traveling lines, Marriage Lines, two two-stitch interlocking traveling cables.*

Figure 8 illustrates three of the more commonly used zig-zagging patterns. From left to right: a column of two adjacent knit stitches; two columns composed of two knit stitches each worked parallel to each other; and two columns composed of two knit stitches intertwining with each other. The cable shown in the middle is often referred to as Marriage Lines, illustrating the ups and downs of married life.

4.3.6 Diamonds and Triangles

Diamonds are some of the most recognizable elements of Aran design. They are a natural extension of zig-zagging lines, as they are simply zig-zag lines placed adjacent to or on top of each other. Like zig-zags, diamonds often benefit from being framed by strongly vertical cables such as ropes or braids.

Diamond shapes lend themselves well to all sorts of variations: they can be filled with moss, seed, rice, or other filler stitches; they can be used singly as an accent; they can be placed adjacent to each other or used in a half-drop formation to create a dramatic center panel; and they combine well with ropes and braids. Triangularly-shaped cables can be formed by working only the bottom half of a diamond pattern, or by working one side of a diamond. Figure 9 shows two basic diamonds. On the left is

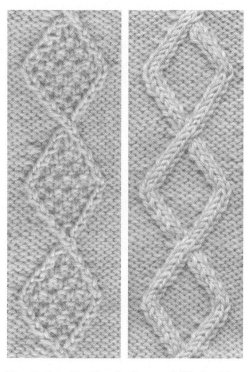

Fig. 9, L to R: *Simple diamond filled with Moss Stitch, two-stitch plain diamond.*

a diamond outlined by a single line of knit stitches (which are twisted on every right-side row) and filled with moss stitch. On the right is a heavier two-stitch diamond outline. All diamond shapes can be varied in size by working more or fewer crosses in one direction before working back in the other direction. Adding intervening plain rows (with no crosses) before changing the direction of the crosses softens the outline of the diamond and creates a slightly rounder shape. Notice that a diamond with a filler stitch has more visual weight than an unfilled diamond.

In Figure 10, a wider panel has been formed by placing two single-diamond motifs adjacent to each other. This larger panel can also be filled — with Garter Stitch, as shown, or with bobbles or other pattern stitches. Where the cable ribs meet, they cross over and under each other to form a trellis pattern.

Fig. 10: *Trellis formed by placing two diamonds adjacent to each other and filling with Garter Stitch.*

Diamonds can also be placed in a half-drop formation. In a half-drop formation, two adjacent motifs have staggered row repeats such that they interlock with each other. The panel shown in Figure 11 is an example of diamonds in a half-drop formation. Notice that the diamonds also have a small rope cable section in place of the simple cross. The individual diamond motif can be lengthened by making the rope cross section even longer.

Working only half of a diamond (either horizontally or vertically) allows the formation of triangle shapes. These shapes, like their diamond parents, can be filled or not, depending upon the desired appearance. They can

Fig. 11: *Diamonds in a half-drop arrangement and filled with Moss Stitch.*

also vary in size depending upon the number of rows worked. Figure 12 shows a triangularly-shaped cable formed by working the bottom half of a diamond cable.

In an Aran design featuring ropes, braids, or softly rounded cable patterns, diamonds are a wonderful addition. Diamonds provide sharper angles that contrast well with softer cable patterns. They are some of the most versatile Aran design elements available. Make use of them!

Fig. 12: *Triangularly-shaped cables formed by working the bottom half of a diamond cable.*

4.3.7 Lace and Cables

Lace in an Aran sweater? At first glance the combination might seem a bit odd—rather like champagne at a BBQ. Used judiciously, though, lace/cable combinations can yield some very striking Aran designs. These designs are particularly nice when worked in lighter-weight wool, cotton, or even silk yarns. (It's hard to envision a lacy Aran in a thick woolen yarn!) Think "dressy Aran" and lace/cable combinations should definitely figure into the design.

Fig. 13, L to R: *A simple rope cable with eyelets, a more complex rope cable/eyelet combination, and a diamond leaf and lace cable.*

Lace/cable combination stitch patterns make up one of the smaller subsets of cable variations. Stitch dictionaries often include only one or two examples. However, adding holes to an existing cable pattern can be done with some advance planning; charts are invaluable. Look for an interval of plain knitting between cabling rows and add eyelets on either side of a center double decrease (Figure 13, left). Traveling lines are excellent places to incorporate a yarn over followed by an SSK or k2tog decrease (Figure 13, middle and right).

Another way to add lace to an Aran design is not within the cables themselves, but between them. Consider using a lace faggoting pattern as the background between cables instead of purl stitches.

4.3.8 Slip-Stitch Cables

One doesn't often see slip-stitch cables in Aran designs. Slip-stitch patterns have a denser row gauge than plain Stockinette Stitch knitting, so it would *seem* overly challenging to try to incorporate them into a design relying mostly on stockinette-based stitch patterns.

In many cases, however, slip-stitch cable patterns have a neglible difference in row gauge compared to surrounding cable patterns. Furthermore, slipping certain stitches allows for light-textured cabling effects which cannot be formed any other way, especially when crossing a single stitch over several stitches.

Figure 14 shows some slip-stitch cable patterns. On the left is Gull Stitch. This stitch pattern forms a small, delicate, wishbone shape, perfect for use as a divider between larger, bolder cables. The middle pattern is the Slipped-Chain Cable and on the right is the Banjo Cable.

As with regular slip-stitch patterns, interesting effects can be achieved with certain slip-stitch cable patterns by changing colors on each right-side row; see the section on Intarsia and Multi-Colored Cables later in this chapter for an example.

Fig. 14, L to R: *Gull Stitch cable, Slipped-Chain Cable, Banjo Cable.*

4.3.9 Closed-Ring Designs

Closed-ring designs (as Barbara Walker refers to them) are cables which arise from within the background stitches instead of being carried up from the start of the work. Rings and other circular designs are possible using this technique, which involves increasing a background stitch or stitches to four, five, or six cable stitches. Barbara Walker's book *Charted Knitting Designs* features quite a few of these cable patterns. Alice Starmore uses them in both *The Celtic Collection* and *Aran Knitting*. Elsebeth Lavold developed her own method for creating these kinds of cable patterns, and they can be found in her book *Viking Patterns for Knitting*.

Fig. 15: *Basic circle cable.*

Barbara Walker's method for creating closed-ring designs involves making a series of increases in and on either side of a center stitch. The number and location of increases made depends upon the size of the cable desired, and whether the bottom of the cable is to be pointed (as for a heart) or round. Figure 15 shows a basic circle cable. Figure 16 shows the more complex Celtic Flourish cable, made up of double interlocking strands, and Figure 17 shows the Celtic Rose Cable, a single motif.

Fig. 16: *Celtic Flourish Cable.*

Fig. 17: *Celtic Rose Cable.*

4.3.10 Ribbed Cables

Interesting textural effects can be achieved by working cable crossings over ribbing patterns. Sometimes the knit stitches within the ribbing are also twisted, to give even more textural interest.

Figure 18 shows two kinds of ribbed cables. On the left is a simple rope cable worked over a k1, p1 ribbing. The knit stitches within this ribbed cable are twisted on every right-side row. On the right is a horseshoe cable worked over a k2, p2 ribbing. In the ribbed rope cable, the stitches maintain their original designation (*e.g.*, either as a knit or as a purl) throughout the crossing maneuvers. In the ribbed horseshoe cable, however, some of the knits change to purls (and vice versa) as the cable crossings are formed.

Figure 19 shows a cable worked over a k2, p2 ribbing for use as a center panel. A cabled ribbing panel such as this one draws in considerably; many more stitches need to be allotted for this kind of stitch pattern than for most other cabled center panels. It is similar to Aran Honeycomb in the way it contracts in width.

Fig. 18, L to R: *A simple ribbed rope cable, a ribbed horseshoe cable.*

The cable shown in Figure 19 is also an example of a ribbed cable which can be worked as a reversible pattern—a desirable characteristic for items such as shawls, scarves, and afghans. In order to make a ribbed cable pattern reversible, the cable crossings involve only the knit ribs on one side of the fabric. The purl stitches separating the knit ribs are removed from the cabling maneuver. Because those purl stitches are the knit ribs on the opposite side of the fabric, however, they are cabled when those rows are worked. It's somewhat analogous to double knitting and great fun to do.

Fig. 19: *A braid panel worked over k2, p2 ribbing.*

4.3.11 Oddball Cables

These cables deserve their own section either because they feature interesting cabling techniques or because they just don't fit into any other category. I guarantee that including one of these cables in your next Aran will provide lots of cabling fun!

Figure 20 shows a variation of the rope cable in which *all* of the stitches to be cabled are placed onto same cable needle, rather than just half of them. The cable needle is then rotated 180° and the stitches are knitted off. If the cable needle is always rotated in the same direction, the result looks similar to a standard rope cable. If the cable needle rotates in different directions on alternate crosses, the result looks more like a wave cable. This cable stands out in slightly sharper relief than a standard cable because the stitches are rotated instead of crossed. This technique also can be applied to other cables which incorporate basic rope and wave crosses.

Fig. 20: *End-Over-End Cable.*

Fig. 21: *Rope cable moving across a reverse stockinette stitch background using a series of increases and decreases on either side of the cable.*

Figure 21 illustrates that it's possible to move a cable across the background stitches while at the same time maintaining its usual cabling pattern. This is accomplished in one of two ways: either stitches in the background fabric are increased and decreased — which causes the fabric and thus the cable to bias — or the cable stitches are moved several extra stitches across the background fabric as they are being cabled (a 2-stitch-over-2-stitch cross would actually take place over six stitches, with the extra 2 stitches being used to move the cable across the background fabric).

Figure 22 illustrates a cabling technique in which half the stitches of the cable are placed on the cable needle, but then stitches are knitted alternately — one from the cable needle and one from the left-hand needle. This technique produces something of a woven

Fig. 22: *Alternating Flat Cable.*

effect in the cable cross. The crossings can be repeated in the same direction to form a rope cable, or in alternate directions to form a wave cable.

Most knitters are familiar with making cables using only one cable needle (or no cable needle at all, if that is your preferred method). Some cable crossings, however, require the use of more than one cable needle. The cable shown in Figure 23 is one example. This cable looks like a strand threaded between the two halves of a wave cable. In order to keep the center cable rib between the two moving cable ribs, some of the knit stitches are placed on one needle and held at the back of the work, and some are placed on another needle and held at the front of the work. This same technique is also used when knitting reversible cable ribbings.

Fig. 23: *Chain-Link Cable.*

Some cables even require that the knitter pass the cable needle from one side of the work to the other (*e.g.*, from front to back or *vice versa*). The cable shown in Figure 24 begins by placing 4 stitches onto a cable needle and holding them at the back of the work. The next stitch is knitted from the left-hand needle, and three of the stitches from the cable needle are replaced onto the left-hand needle. Before working those three replaced stitches, however, the knitter must pass the cable needle with its single remaining stitch from the back of the work to the front. The next three stitches are knitted from the left-hand needle followed by the last stitch on the cable needle.

Fig. 24: *Coin Cable.*

4.3.12 Smocked Cables

Sometimes known as cluster stitches, smocked cables are ones where the yarn is wrapped one or more times around groups of cable ribs to draw them together. This may be done for structural reasons —to draw the ribs together instead of crossing them—for decorative purposes, or both (Figure 25).

Smocked cables make interesting center panels and can also be used on the bodice of a sweater to imitate the look of a smocked woven fabric.

Fig. 25: *Smocked cable pattern used as a center panel.*

4.3.13 Embellished Cables

Some of the prettiest Aran designs I've seen incorporated some form of embellishment. The most common embellishment is embroidery, in one of several forms. The cable itself can be highlighted with decorative stitching in the same or contrasting colors (see Figure 26), or the embroidery can be used to decorate the plain areas between the cables.

Cables can also be embellished with beads, paillettes, and other decorative elements. Beads can be placed within the cable or along the edges of it (see Figure 27).

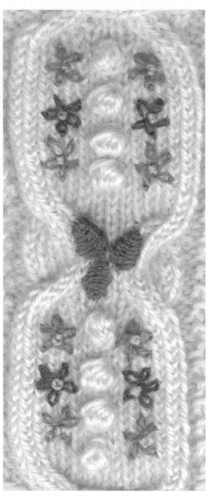

Fig. 26: *A cable embellished with embroidery.*

Fig. 27: *A cable embellished with glass beads.*

4.3.14 Intarsia and Multi-Colored Cables

Aran designs need not be limited to single colors. Using the techniques of intarsia and slip-stitch knitting, all sorts of multi-colored effects can be incorporated into an Aran design. Here are just a few examples.

Novice intarsia knitters may want to start by knitting an example like the one shown in Figure 28. In this swatch, each cable panel is knitted in a different color.

Fig. 28: *Aran sweater design incorporating three different colors of yarn.*

Five bobbins or butterflies of yarn are used, one for each panel. Here the panels are arranged symmetrically, but a very dramatic Aran might be knit using this method, with the panels arranged asymmetrically. The colors used could contrast sharply, or be gradations of the same color for a more subtle effect. These intarsia panels are especially effective when a tweedy or heathered yarn is used.

Figure 29 shows a plait in which each strand is knitted in a different color. The background is a fourth color. Knitting this cable requires five bobbins or butterflies of yarn: two of the background color (one for either side of the cable), and one each of the three colors used in the plait. The colors change as each strand is knitted. It's a fairly easy technique that provides a lot of visual impact. The most difficult part of knitting this kind of cable is keeping the yarn bobbins from tangling.

Those knitters looking for a challenge might want to consider knitting an Aran in which each of the cable panels is composed of knitted ribs traveling over a purled background (rather than solid cables such as ropes or horsehoes). The background could be a solid, contrasting color; very dramatic effects are achieved when a solid color is used for

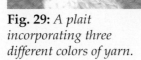

Fig. 29: *A plait incorporating three different colors of yarn.*

the cable and a coordinating variegated yarn is used for the background. An example of such a cable is shown in Figure 30. These are more complicated intarsia patterns than the previous examples because they require many more bobbins. A braid panel, for example, would require a bobbin for each individual strand within the braid. It is possible to use a single bobbin for the cable ribs and do some stranding across the back of the work, but this often makes it more difficult to achieve an even gauge and makes the fabric bulkier.

Changing colors on alternate rows of a slip-stitch cable pattern is a very easy way to add color to an Aran design. In the example in Figure 31, Color A is used to work rows 1 and 2, and Color B is used to work rows 3 and 4. As with the other examples shown, the yarns can be two contrasting solids, or one solid and one variegated.

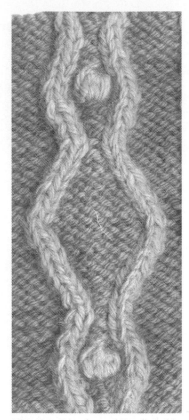

Fig. 30: *Ripple and Rock Cable worked in a contrasting color from the background.*

Fig. 31: *Slip-stitch diamond pattern with Colors A and B worked on alternate rows.*

4.4 Other Aran Design Elements

Cables aren't the only stitch elements found in Aran sweaters. Other three-dimensional texture stitches contribute to the overall sculptured effect of these designs.

4.4.1 Twisted Stitches and Stitches That Twist

What is the difference? Twisted stitches are individual stitches knitted through the back of the loop so that the loop twists (see Figure 32). Twisting the loop causes it to stand away from the background, a useful characteristic when one wants sharp lines within a design. Some stitch patterns call for stitches to be twisted on right-side rows; some call for them to be twisted on every row. Twisting stitches on every row causes them to stand out in very sharp relief. However, doing so can also cause the fabric to bias or be very stiff.

Fig. 32: *Twisted knit stitches within a cable.*

Stitches that twist, on the other hand, are stitches which move across the background one or sometimes two stitches at a time (see Figure 33). These kinds of stitches are quite similar in appearance to simple cable crosses, although they are usually worked without a cable needle. Be aware, though, that different methods for working these crosses result in subtly different appearances to these stitches, which can impact the look of the fabric. Barbara Walker notes in *A Second Treasury of Knitting Patterns* that "The standard method of working a Right Twist is: skip 1 st, knit the second st, then knit the skipped st and sl both sts from needle together. The standard method of working a Left Twist is: skip 1 st and knit the second st in back loop, then knit the skipped st in front loop and sl both sts from needle together. . . . These methods, however, are not 'standard' in this book. Both twists can be done in a better way—at least in this author's opinion." She goes on to suggest that her readers try the alternate method for working Left and Right Twists as given in the glossary of *A Second Treasury of Knitting Patterns*.

My own experience indicates that the "standard" method of working a Right Twist

Fig. 33: *Stitches that twist across a background of stockinette stitch.*

results in a cross that—because of the path the yarn travels—"humps up" from the base of the knitting. Personally, I find its appearance less attractive than that of Barbara Walker's alternative Right Twist, worked as follows: K2tog leaving stitches on left-hand needle, then insert right-hand needle between the two stitches just knitted and knit the first stitch again, then slip both stitches from left-hand needle.

I break with Barbara Walker when working the Left Twist, however, as I find that the original method is faster and the difference in appearance is negligible. Her alternative Left Twist is worked as follows: With right-hand needle behind left-hand needle, skip one stitch and knit the second stitch in back loop, then insert right-hand needle into the backs of *both* stitches (the skipped stitch and the second stitch) and k2 together through back loops.

Note that these instructions apply only to Right and Left Twists worked on the public side of the fabric. A stitch pattern occasionally may specify Right and Left Twists on the private side of the fabric as well. A Right Purl Twist on the private side of the fabric will produce a Right Twist on the public side of the fabric. It is worked as follows: With yarn in front, skip the first stitch and purl the second stitch, then purl the skipped stitch, then slip both stitches from needle together. A Left Purl Twist on the private side of the fabric will produce a Left Twist on the public side of the fabric.

It is worked as follows: Bring the right-hand needle behind the first stitch on the left-hand needle, purl into the second stitch on the left-hand needle, then the first stitch, then drop both from left-hand needle.

At the risk of further confusion, I note also that variations of the maneuvers detailed above allow the knitter to make Left and Right Twists which incorporate purl stitches (*e.g.*, a single knit stitch crosses over a purl stitch rather than another knit stitch). The instructions for working these kinds of crosses usually accompany the stitch pattern directions.

These two techniques of working twisted stitches and stitches that twist can be combined, creating cable lines which stand out in sharp relief (see Figure 34). This type of knitting is often known as "Bavarian" or "Austrian" because it is prevelent in those areas of the world. These crosses must be worked carefully to ensure that the stitches being twisted and crossed are not stretched out of shape, resulting in a sloppy appearance to the cable.

Fig. 34. *Bavarian twisted stitch braid panel.*

4.4.2 Trims

The standard k1, p1 or k2, p2 ribbings on Aran sweaters aren't the only options for trims. Many kinds of ribbings and welts make suitable trims. The choice of which to use depends upon the desired look of the garment.

Vertically oriented ribbing, composed primarily of columns of knits flanked by columns of purls, do not curl and often provide some stretch. A pattern such as k1, p1 ribbing stretches and contracts easily, making it a good choice for place where the garment needs to cling to the body.

Fig. 35: *Right-Twist Rib.*

Swatching a pattern will help to determine if the chosen ribbing pattern will be decorative (a bobble rib, for example), or functional (a twisted rib). Often, a ribbing pattern can be carried up into the body of the sweater.

Figure 35 shows one of the simplest variations on plain k2, p2 ribbing. In this stitch pattern, the columns of knit stitches are twisted on each right-side row. Two purl stitches separate the columns of knit stitches.

Fig. 36: *Rick-Rack Rib.*

Some Aran designs feature a "skirt," instead of ribbing. A skirt is a non-elastic bottom edging—usually 6" deep or more—in patterning which contrasts or coordinates with the body fabric. The ribbing pattern shown in Figure 36 is not very elastic, making it the perfect choice for a skirt or other trim which isn't intended to draw in close to the body.

A skirt on an Aran sweater is usually set off from the body patterning by a welt of Garter Stitch or some other horizontal pattern. Horizontally oriented welts, such as Garter Stitch, resist curling. If the gauge between the skirt and the body patterning differs, compensating increases or decreases may be necessary.

4.4.3 Filler Stitches

Filler stitches are simple, small-repeat stitch patterns often composed of just knits and purls. They provide backgrounds for the cable patterns and act as "fillers" for spaces where cables either wouldn't be seen or are not desired (along the sides of sweaters, for instance).

Reverse Stockinette Stitch is the traditional background stitch for cable patterns. It recedes into the background and helps to emphasize the cable patterns. However, don't reject the possibility of using other kinds of backgrounds. Cables on a

Fig. 37: *Seed Stitch.*

background of Garter Stitch are texturally interesting. A single cable repeated over a background of Seed Stitch (Figure 37) or Moss Stitch (Figure 38) is elegant and lovely. Swatching is a must when using a background other than Reverse Stockinette Stitch, as the fabric may not contract as much.

Fig. 38: *Moss Stitch.*

Although Seed Stitch and Moss Stitch are traditional Aran sweater filler stitches, many other knit/purl combinations work well, too. Other texture stitches such as basketweave, Trinity Stitch, and Rice Stitch (Figure 39) work are fun to work and will add a unique touch to your design.

Sometimes the names of stitch patterns can be confusing: the stitch that is called Seed Stitch in the United States is often referred to as Moss Stitch in the United Kingdom. Sand Stitch is very similar to Rice Stitch; both patterns have one row of k1, p1 ribbing followed by a row of knitting. The difference is that in Rice Stitch, the knit stitches in the row of k1, p1 are twisted; in Sand Stitch, they are not.

The most important requirement for a good filler stitch is that it have a row gauge compatible with

Fig. 39: *Rice Stitch.*

the cable patterns; slip-stitch patterns probably won't work very well because of the differing row gauges.

4.4.4 Knots, Bobbles, and Popcorn Stitches

Knots, bobbles, and popcorn stitches add lots of three-dimensional texture to designs. It's easy to get carried away and "overbobble" a design, so remember that these elements are best used judiciously (although I once designed a sweater that had 533 bobbles on it, and it turned out beautifully). Because they also require extra manipulation of the knitting, you may find it tedious to work large numbers of them.

I define knots as those raised textural elements which are worked on only one row. An example is a knot which is made by working (k1, p1, k1, p1, k1) into a stitch to make five stitches out of one, then passing the 2nd, 3rd, 4th, and 5th stitches, one at a time, over the first one. Figure 40 shows the use of such a knot within a cable pattern.

Fig. 40: *Briar Rose Cable.*

Gordian knots (see Barbara Walker's *Second Treasury of Knitting Patterns*) are formed by making a specific kind of cable crossing, rather than by increasing and decreasing stitches. Gordian knots are used to create a decorative cable crossing where two cable ribs meet, as in Figure 41. Where the cable ribs come together, they cross in such a way that a raised purl knot is formed between them.

Fig. 41: *Cable pattern incorporating Gordian Knots.*

Bobbles, in contrast to knots, are raised textural elements worked separately from the background fabric over an additional number of rows. Bobbles can be smooth (by working the bobble in Stockinette Stitch) or textured (by working the bobble in Garter or even Seed Stitch). Figure 42 illustrates smooth and textured bobbles.

The question I hear most often regarding bobbles is "How can I make nice round bobbles which stay on the surface of the fabric?" A variety of methods exist; see Chapter 7, "Useful Knitting Tips" for some tips for better bobbles.

Popcorn stitches are pattern stitches which

Fig. 42: *Bobbles, smooth and textured.*

produce a bumpy, raised, or otherwise heavily
textured surface. These stitches have many uses
in Aran designs: as center panels, accent panels,
as filler stitches for the sides of a design, and as
filler stitches within diamonds and other cables.
The best-known of these stitches is Trinity Stitch
(so called because the process of forming this
stitch requires the knitter to make three stitches
from one and one stitch from three), shown
in Figure 43. It is also known as Blackberry
Stitch because it does resemble blackberries.
The interesting thing about Trinity Stitch is
that—unlike most stitch patterns—all the action
happens on wrong-side rows. Right-side rows

Fig. 43: *Trinity Stitch.*

are simply purled; all increasing and decreasing happens on the wrong side of the
work.

Fig. 44: *Star Stitch.*

Trinity Stitch used to be one of my least-
favorite stitch patterns, but I've found that the
key to working this stitch pattern is to have
needles with very sharp tips. I prefer needles
with sharp tips for most of my knitting. Blunt-
tipped needles make it more difficult to work
the three-stitch-to-one decrease. Now that I
know that little secret, Trinity Stitch has become
one of my favorite stitch patterns.

Star Stitch (Figure 44) is similar to Trinity
Stitch in that it is also formed by increasing
three stitches from one and decreasing three
stitches to one. It forms a stiffer fabric with a
slightly flatter surface than Trinity Stitch.

Creating a Design 5

We've all heard it said (maybe you've said it yourself!): "Oh, I could never design a sweater! I'm just not creative!"

I don't believe that. I used to, but not anymore.

I am convinced that a form of creativity can be learned by those of us who weren't lucky enough to be born with an abundance of natural talent. It has taken me several decades but I have finally learned to live in both sides of my brain. I have always been most comfortable with the left side of my brain. As long as I have structure, organization, and rules to follow, I do very well. I remember wistfully thinking that it would be nice to be able to tap into the other side of my brain and "be creative," but I never knew quite how to do it. I envied those people who could picture something in their heads and turn it into reality.

Knitting is a lot like music (one of my other passions). Mozart "heard" entire symphonies in his head and simply transcribed them onto a piece of paper. Some designers "see" the finished product in their mind's eye and only need knitting needles and yarn to transform their vision into a finished product. I have very limited spatial perception (ask my husband about the placement of light switches and wall outlets in our house), so I had to figure out another way to "be creative."

I've found that it's easiest for me to be creative if I first establish a set of parameters for myself within which I am free to explore. It's very difficult for me to flip through a stitch dictionary and predict what cable combinations will look good together unless I subconsciously categorize them—by geometric shape, by row repeat, by visual weight, *etc.* Because I lack the ability to know, instinctively, what I want the end result to look like, I design by working within an artificial set of "rules" that I have created for myself. It's no different than a musician learning music theory—the set of rules that govern music and musical creativity.

It's important to point out that I am not advocating that my way of designing is the best way, or the only way. I use it only to illustrate that designing is within the grasp of all of us—it's just that some of us have to go about it differently than others because of the way our brains are wired.

Something I found tremendously helpful when I first started designing was to analyze existing Aran designs. Page through knitting magazines and pattern books. Look at the designs. If you find one you like, try to determine what it is that makes it so appealing. Is it the combination of patterns? Is it the unique use of a pattern or patterns? Is it the placement of the patterns in the design?

If you find a design you don't like, do the same thing. What could you change about that design to make it more appealing? These mental gymnastics aren't designed to enable you to copy other people's designs, but rather to help you avoid the pitfalls that can occur when you start designing your own Arans.

5.1 Planning the Cable Layout

One of the most difficult aspects of designing an Aran sweater is the need to juggle many different parts of the design simultaneously. Not only must you consider the choice and placement of the cables, you also must consider how they affect the size of the garment; where they begin and end in relation to the garment shaping; and technical details such as cable splay and row repeat compatibility. Overcoming these challenges does become easier with each design.

5.1.1 Body Measurements

Step one is to identify the target measurements of the final garment, because those measurements—especially the width at the chest—will tell you how much real estate is available in which to fit the cable patterns. You can take the actual body measurements of the intended wearer and add the desired amount of ease (extra width added for comfort and style). I've found, however, that taking the measurements from an existing sweater which fits the wearer well and is knit from the same weight of yarn is a good place to start. Do this for a few of your own sweaters and you may be surprised by the results. For instance, I used to believe that I liked sweaters with roomy armhole openings, so I always made my armhole depths 9-10". However, after measuring a few commercially-knit sweaters in my wardrobe, I discovered that the ones I really liked the best had armhole depths of only 7-8".

5.1.2 Design Balance

Designing an Aran isn't merely a matter of opening a stitch dictionary, picking out three or four cable patterns you like and throwing them together in your design. Such a random approach to designing could lead to some unpleasant surprises. And while there isn't one "magic formula" which governs the layout of the cable patterns, there are some helpful guidelines. These guidelines can aid you in achieving a result that is much more than the sum of its parts.

An attractive Aran design balances horizontally across its pattern layout and vertically in the row repeats of its pattern. This balance is critical. Many a great Aran design has been ruined by a cable that just doesn't fit or one that stops mid-repeat at a critical place such as the neckline. However, don't let "analysis paralysis" prevent you from forging ahead with a design idea. Be prepared to swatch and refine as you go along.

Eventually you will find that you need to rely on these guidelines less and less, and you'll even begin to look for opportunities to "break the rules." Your imagination is the limit.

It might seem daunting at first to have to remember all these details as you begin to select patterns for your design. I doubt the knitters of the earliest Aran sweaters took all these factors into consideration, but I have given them to you to use in the hope that they will help you avoid a lot of frustration and ripping out.

5.1.2.1 A Bit of Math

Let's examine the "traditional" Aran sweater layout, one with a central cable panel flanked by narrower cable panels. Part of the reason that this layout is aesthetically pleasing is the "golden ratio" and it deserves a bit of explanation here. Alice Korach described this concept nicely as it relates to Aran and Fair Isle designs in her article "A Balancing Act: Knitter's Guide to Pattern and Proportion," in *Threads Magazine*. I will summarize the basic idea here. Even if you consider yourself mathematically challenged, take a moment to try to understand the principle behind it.

Shown below is a line 13 cm long.

_____

Now we will cut this line into two segments, one 8 cm long and one 5 cm long, like this:

_____

_____

If we divide the length of the first line (13 cm) by the length of the longer of the two cut lines (8 cm), we get the number 1.625. And if we divide the length of the longer of the two cut lines by the length of the shorter one (8 cm divided by 5 cm), we get the number 1.6 (which for our purposes is close enough to 1.625). For some reason, the human brain finds elements related by this golden ratio to be aesthetically pleasing — the architecture of Greek temples follows this principle.

An extension of the golden ratio is the Fibonacci sequence. The sequence is a series of numbers beginning with 1. The next number in the sequence is also 1, and each number after that is the sum of the two previous numbers. Therefore, the sequence is 1, 1, 2, 3, 5, 8, 13...and so on. As numbers are added to the sequence, the ratio of any two successive numbers gets closer and closer to the golden ratio.

The Fibonacci sequence has all sorts of useful applications in designing. Choose cable patterns whose widths are the same measurements as numbers in the Fibonacci sequence, and you will be well on your way to finding cable patterns which harmonize well with each other (width is not the only consideration, though, as we will see). For instance, let's say you are making a sweater which is 42" around. There is 21" on both the front and back in which to lay out the cable patterns. The choices might include a center cable pattern which is 5" wide, flanked by two cables which are 2" wide, flanked by two outside cables which are 3" wide, with a knit-purl pattern filling in the remaining space on each side.

One of the nice things about the Fibonacci sequence is that it's okay to use the numbers out of sequence. Thus, the 3" wide patterns don't have to be right next to the 5" wide pattern. Also, the patterns don't have to be exactly 2", 3", or 5" wide. Your eye won't be able to tell if a center panel is 4½" or 5½" wide, so don't drive yourself nuts over it.

If all this math stifles your creativity, ignore it. I offer it for those people who like to have guidelines to follow in unfamiliar territory. A design is not going to "fail" because it doesn't follow the correct mathematical principles; as we shall see, many elements contribute to a successful Aran design.

5.1.2.2 Scale

Scale here refers to the size of the cable patterns in relation to the size of the garment. Generally speaking, the larger the garment, the larger and more dramatic the cable patterns can be. A bold cable pattern might overwhelm a sweater for a small child, and it simply may not fit within the available stitch count (although you can circumvent this problem by making the sweater with a very lightweight yarn). Likewise, you probably wouldn't make a sweater for a man with small, delicate, lacy patterning.

5.1.2.3 Sibling Rivalry—or Why Some Patterns Get Along and Some Don't

Selecting a group of cable patterns which compliment each other is, I think, the single most difficult aspect of designing an Aran sweater. Every other aspect of the design could be planned down to the smallest detail, but if the cable patterns don't harmonize well, the design may not be successful. Where then, to begin?

When I design, I often have an idea in mind: I may have sketched out some cable patterns to see how they will look together (I do this when talking on the phone). Sometimes my idea is more nebulous, and I look for inspiration in the patterns themselves. A cable pattern may incorporate bobbles or a textural stitch which lead to ideas for the rest of the layout.

Stitch patterns have personalities: some are bold and dramatic, some are shy and retiring. Some are complex and some have simple beauty. Some are angular and geometric, some are round and flowing. These characteristics can help you in choosing patterns which will look good together in a design.

Variation in characteristics is necessary for a good design; if you choose cables which have too may characteristics in common, you could end up with a visually boring layout. At the same time, though, you don't want the layout to be scattered and uncoordinated.

Let's consider a traditional layout, one with a center panel flanked by narrower panels on either side. I usually begin by choosing a center panel; the remaining cable patterns are selected on the basis of how they coordinate with the center panel. When choosing the coordinating cables, keep these ideas in mind:

- If the center panel is a diamond pattern with angular lines, you might place a "rounder" cable pattern to either side of it. Then you might add a narrow braid cable to add a bit of textural interest.

- Consider the "density" of the pattern, or how much of the background shows through the cable. An openwork diamond is going to appear much less dense than a horseshoe cable, for example. You'll want to include both types of patterns in your design. The denser patterns also have a more strongly vertical appearance, and that characteristic can be useful if you want them to "frame" other patterns in the design. Ropes and braids are excellent choices to frame a center panel with uneven edges, such as a diamond or a trellis.

- While a certain amount of variation in the size and width of patterns is desirable, it's not usually a good idea to mix very heavy and very light cable patterns in your design. A heavy braid pattern may overwhelm the feathery-looking trellis pattern next to it.

- Columns of twisted knit stitches, or narrow two-stitch cables, do double duty in Aran designs. They are useful for setting cable patterns off from one another, and they also act as "spacers." If you have enough major cable patterns in your design, but have extra stitches to use up, you can place some of these smaller spacer cables between patterns. It's not absolutely necessary to include them in a design, though. Cable patterns separated only by purl stitches have a more subtle appearance which is just as pleasing.

- Many cables incorporate Seed Stitch, Moss Stitch, twisted stitches, or other kinds of textural patterns. They can make an ordinary design outstanding. And one of my favorite techniques is to place cables on a textured background — Rice, Moss, Garter, Seed, or another texture stitch makes a great background, especially for bold cables.

Swatching is going to give you a good idea of the visual "weight" of each cable pattern and — more importantly — how the patterns look in combination with each other. You can also use the "copy machine" method, in which you photocopy pictures of the stitch patterns, then cut them up and move them around until you find a pleasing arrangement. This is a good preliminary method, but not a substitute for swatching.

By the way, the cable patterns don't have to be identical on the front and back of your sweater. You can use two different center panels on the front and the back, or the same center panel on the front and back but different flanking cables. If you want to make a cardigan instead of a pullover, you probably will need to modify the center front panel. Use a different, narrower panel on either side of the front opening, choose a center panel for the back which can be split down the middle, or use a filler stitch in place of the center cable panel.

As you familiarize yourself with your stitch dictionaries, the process of choosing cable patterns for an Aran design will become easier. I have a few favorite cables which seem to work in just about any design, but I also try to throw in a couple of new and different ones to keep things interesting. And I often find that when I'm working on one garment, I'll be designing two or three others at the same time, simply because I see so many patterns I want to use.

5.1.2.4 The Layout

Assigning a letter designation to each cable in the design helps me arrange the overall layout. For example, in a design which has three different cables (A, B, and C), the layout might look like this:

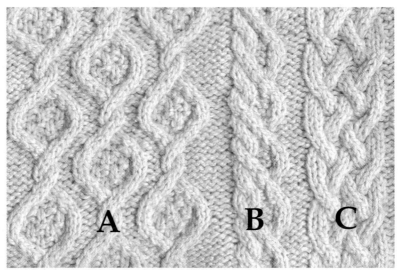

Fig. 45: *Cable layout using three different cable patterns.*

The following layout also uses only three different cables (also A, B, and C), but one of them is used twice:

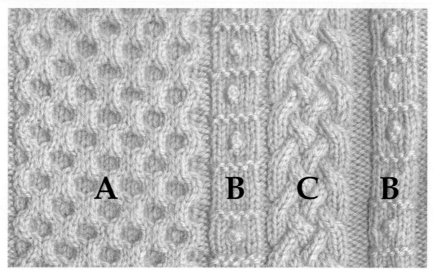

Fig. 46: *Cable layout also using three different cable patterns, one of which is used twice.*

The third layout is the most complex, and includes four cables (A, B, C, and D); two of the cable patterns are used twice:

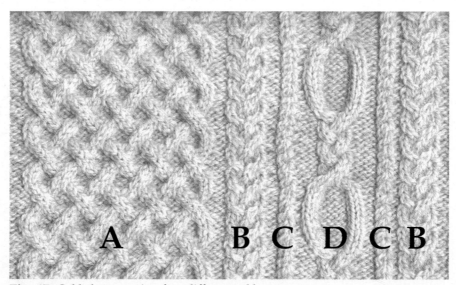

Fig. 47: *Cable layout using four different cable patterns.*

These layouts illustrate three of the most common arrangements of cables in an Aran sweater. They are based largely on the principles of the golden ratio and cable compatibility discussed earlier in this chapter. These are by no means the only options. Asymmetric layouts can also be pleasing, as can even more complex symmetrical ones.

5.1.2.5 Row Repeats

Once you've considered the placement of cable patterns across the width of the sweater, it's time to examine the impact of their row repeats. I never used to consider row repeats of patterns or even my row gauge to be of any significance, but they have important (and sometimes unexpected) effects on Aran designs.

Compatibility. If you are designing your first Aran sweater, I advise you to pick cables patterns with compatible row repeats. The chart at right can help you by showing you what repeats are compatible with the largest row repeat in your design. For instance, if the cable with the largest row repeat is 32 rows, then any cable with row repeats of 2, 4, 8, or 16 rows will also be compatible.

Why are compatible repeats so important? It's not an inflexible rule—it's quite possible to use patterns with incompatible row repeats successfully—but it's a useful guideline, for a couple of reasons:

• It's harder to keep track of your place in the overall design if one pattern repeats every six rows, another every fourteen rows, and a third one every twenty rows. It can be done, especially if you've managed to memorize the cable patterns and can "see" the cables develop as you knit. For novice Aran knitters and designers, though, compatible repeats make for easier knitting.

• Many cables "swing," or move from right to left and back again. If you place a cable which swings every six rows next to one which swings every ten rows, you will have cables swinging out of sync with each other (see Figure 49). It would be like you and

Largest Row Repeat	Compatible Row Repeats
8	2, 4
12	2, 4, 6
16	2, 4, 8
18	2, 6
20	2, 4, 10
24	2, 4, 6, 8, 12
28	2, 4, 14
30	2, 6, 10
32	2, 4, 8, 16
36	2, 4, 6, 12, 18
40	2, 4, 8, 10, 20
44	2, 4, 22
48	2, 4, 6, 8, 12, 24

Fig. 48: *Chart listing compatible cable patterns by row repeat.*

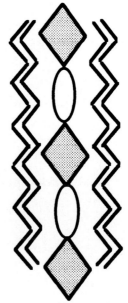

Fig. 49: *Out of sync cables which have incompatible row repeats.*

your partner trying to dance, except you're doing a waltz and he's doing the two-step. If you want to use two cables with incompatible row repeats and you want to avoid this problem, don't place them right next to each other in the design.

With a little help from your calculator, it is possible to use cable patterns with incompatible repeats and avoid the problem of fractions of cable patterns in the design. For instance, if you have selected cable patterns for your design which have repeats of 8, 10, and 12 rows, by the time you've reached the 10th repeat of the 12-row pattern, the other two patterns will be in sync with it (12 rows x 10 repeats = 120 rows, and 120 is evenly divisible by both 8 and 10). If each 12-row repeat measures 2", 10 repeats would result in a sweater measuring 20" without ribbing.

Some row repeats have many compatible repeats, and some have fewer compatible repeats. If the largest row repeat in the design is 24 rows, then you can select from cable patterns with row repeats of 2, 4, 6, 8, and 12 rows. If the largest row repeat in the design is 18 rows, however, the only compatible cable patterns are ones with repeats of 2 or 6 rows. That could severely limit the choice of patterns for the design. But—once again—a little creative mathematics can ease the way. Let's say you wanted to use a cable pattern with a repeat of 28 rows in the design. The cable repeat measures 4" in the knitted swatch, so these are some of your design options:

• Knitting four repeats of a 28-row cable pattern results in a sweater which is 16" long without ribbing—a length which is a bit short for most adults, but which could work well in a child's design. Four repeats of a 28-row cable pattern equals 112 total rows, and 112 is also divisible by 2, 4, 8, 14, and 16, so cable patterns with those row repeats would fit well into the finished design.

• Knitting five repeats of a 28-row cable pattern results in a sweater which is 20" long without ribbing. This is a better length for most adult sweaters. Five repeats of a 28-row pattern equals 140 total rows. Therefore, cables with row repeats of 2, 4, 10, 14, and 20 rows would fit well into the finished design.

• Knitting six repeats of a 28-row cable pattern results in a sweater which is 24" long without ribbing. Six repeats of a 28-row pattern equals 168 rows, which means that cables with repeats of 2, 4, 6, 8, 12, 14, and 24 rows would fit well into the finished design.

Vertically Asymmetrical Patterns. These kinds of cable patterns require careful placement in a design. Figure 50 shows what can happen when a vertically asymmetrical pattern is used.

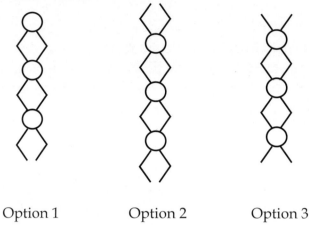

Option 1   Option 2   Option 3

Fig. 50: *Options for placing a vertically asymmetrical pattern in a design.*

Option 1 is an example of a vertically asymmetrical cable. Using three complete repeats of the cable pattern in your design would give it an unbalanced look. In this case, there are two solutions. Option 2, shown in the middle, is to add another half of the repeat. This method is acceptable, but it lengthens the original design. That may or may not be okay, depending upon what finished length is desired. Option 3, shown on the right, splits the original repeat, which maintains the original length but balances the pattern. Use the patterns as given in stitch dictionaries as starting points, but feel free to begin the pattern at a different place in the repeat in order to make it fit well into the design.

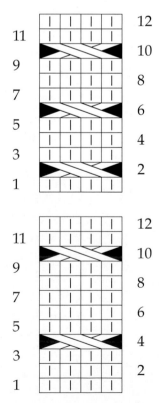

Altering Row Repeats. It's also possible to change the row repeat of a cable pattern—making the cable crossings happen sooner or later in the pattern—in order to make it compatible with other cables in the design. It's easier to visualize these possible changes when you're working from charts, as in Figures 51 and 52. Figure 51 shows a change from a 4-stitch rope cable which crosses to the left every fourth row to the same cable which crosses to the left every sixth row. Figure 52 shows how the same cable pattern can be worked over a different number of rows—in this example, either 16 rows or 24 rows.

Fig. 51: *Altering row repeats to make them fit into a design.*

Fig. 52: *A cable pattern originally worked over 16 rows and 32 stitches changed to 24 rows and 44 stitches.*

5.1.3 Cable Splay

"Cable splay" is a phenomenon that occurs at the transition of a cable pattern into another stitch pattern, such as ribbing. The gauges of the two stitch patterns differ to such an extent that the fabric itself is distorted.

The swatch in Figure 53 illustrates this problem. Notice that at the point where the Seed Stitch border ends and the cable begins, the cable "splays" out, distorting the bottom edge of the swatch. The top edge of the swatch, where the cable transitions into the Seed Stitch border, is also distorted. This phenomenon can happen whenever there is a transition from one pattern (*e.g.*, ribbing, Stockinette, Seed Stitch) into a cable pattern. Some cable patterns suffer from this problem more than others (you'll be able to tell from your swatch). You can compensate for it in one or both of two ways:

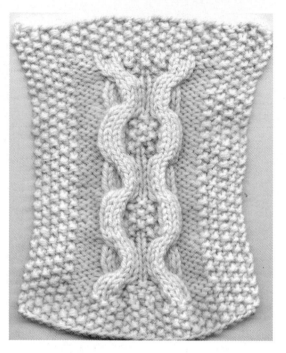

Fig. 53: *Cable splay.*

Fig. 54: *Adjusting for cable splay with increases and decreases at the transition points.*

1. Increase at the base of any cable wider than four stitches. How many increases should you make? An increase stitch or two at the base of each cable should eliminate the problem. When you reach the other end of the piece, make the corresponding decrease(s).

2. Make sure there is a cable crossing on the first or second right-side row after you begin the cable pattern. This is a good practice to follow even when cable splay isn't an issue, as it looks more polished.

Figure 54 shows a swatch where cable splay has been minimized using both of the methods discussed above.

5.1.4 Vertical Placement

The vertical placement of a cable within a design is visually important. Avoid "chopping off" a cable in mid-repeat at the top or bottom of a garment. It is most important to have complete repeats of the pattern with the largest row repeat (which is often, but not always, the center panel). Any design with fractions of cable patterns — particularly the center cable pattern — below the wearer's face is visually jarring. If it's necessary to have fractions of cables because of incompatible row repeats, plan the design so that they occur just above the ribbing. They will be less noticeable there than they would be at the top of the sweater.

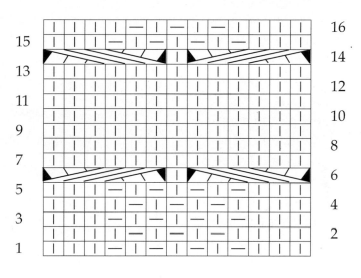

It's always worth looking at what row the cable pattern begins on, both for cable splay and aesthetic reasons. This is easiest to do when working from charts. A cable stitch might just look better if it begins in a different place in the pattern, as in the following example.

Figure 55 shows charts for the cable pattern known as Medallion Moss Cable. This is the pattern shown in the swatch illustrating cable splay. In the swatch, this cable is worked from the chart shown on the top, and begins with half a circle. If

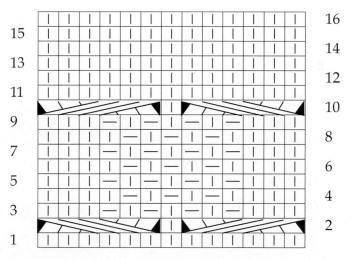

Fig. 55: *Adjusting charts so that cable patterns begin with a crossing row.*

rows 11-16 are moved to the bottom of the chart, as shown on the bottom chart, there will be a cable crossing on the 2nd right-side row (which will help to minimize the cable splay), and the pattern will begin with a full circle.

5.1.5 Cable Orientation

Many cable patterns are bidirectional and don't appear different when knitted top-down instead of bottom-up. However, some cable patterns are unidirectional; in order for them to have the correct orientation in a top-down design, the chart/pattern needs to be adjusted.

Figure 56 shows two charts for a variation of the Valentine Cable from Barbara Walker's *A Treasury of Knitting Patterns*. The top chart is similar to the pattern as given; however, in a top-down design, the heart would appear upside-down. Using the bottom chart will ensure that the heart has the proper orientation in the design. Note also that the chart on the top begins with a right-side row; the chart on the bottom begins with a wrong-side row. This is a situation where using charts gives a very clear visual picture of what's happening with the cable pattern and where adjustments might need to be made.

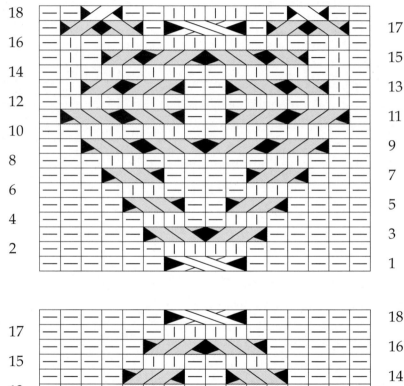

Fig. 56: *Charts for knitting the same motif bottom-up (upper chart) and top-down (lower chart).*

5.2 Creative Options

Sometimes it is difficult to find a center cable panel which is wide enough for the design (remember, a center panel should be between 5"-8" wide, depending upon the size of the garment). It is possible to combine cable patterns in order to "build" a suitable center panel. Here are some ideas:

Select a narrower pattern and
repeat it three times for a center panel.

Repeat a narrower pattern three times,
as above, but turn the center cable
upside down.

Use a half-drop formation, placing
the second multiple of a cable next to
the first but moving it up or down
by half the cable's rows.

Use a "filler stitch" (such as
Trinity stitch) as the center panel.

Place two repeats of the same cable
pattern side-by-side.

5.3 Using "Unique" Cable Patterns

Many cable patterns just don't fit into a traditional Aran design. Some of them have
very large row repeats. Some of them are so bold and aggressive that they overwhelm
other patterns in the design. Those are the patterns which are often perfect for a less
traditional Aran design. The legendary Enchanted Aran Forest cardigan by Donna
Karan, which appeared in the Fall 1992 issue of *Vogue Knitting*, is a perfect example
of such a design. It has several cabled tree patterns around the bottom of the sweater,
patterns which would have been difficult to place in a traditional layout but which work
beautifully in this design. Having trouble placing a cable in a design? Try one of these
ideas:

Use a multiple of the cable and
repeat it around the entire sweater.

Alternate two cable patterns—one wide,
one narrow—around the entire sweater.

Use it as a single center cable.
Place it on a textured background,
or fill it with Moss, Garter, or Seed Stitch.

Use it as a single motif—for example, the
Two Trees pattern from Barbara Walker's
*A Second Treasury of Knitting
Patterns*.

Putting It All Together 6

Designing an Aran involves keeping track of lots of different details. By now you're probably thinking that it would be easier just to get out the latest knitting magazine and knit an Aran design for which someone else did all the work. Think of the sense of accomplishment you'll have, though, if you persevere and design your own unique garment! And by doing as much advance planning as possible, you'll avoid nasty surprises halfway into knitting the design.

6.1 Swatching

Yes, I know there are knitters who can knit without ever having to swatch. They are the ones who snort disdainfully at we knitters who "waste" time and materials knitting gauge swatches. I also know that most knitters don't like to knit gauge swatches. We'd all like to get to the fun part of knitting the actual sweater! However, swatching does more than allow you to determine your basic stitch gauge.

• It allows you to determine the gauge of the individual cable patterns in the design.

• It allows you to see how they will look when placed next to each other in the garment.

• It allows you to anticipate any growth or shrinkage in the yarn—and thus the completed garment—in advance. It's always a good idea to wash and block your gauge swatch just as you plan to wash and block the finished garment.

• It will allow you to determine your row gauge, and thus the vertical measurements of the cable repeats.

• It will allow you to see if you even like knitting the pattern, or if you'd prefer to work it with a different kind of needle.

• It allows you to accumulate a library of patterns. Think of the swatches as puzzle pieces—you can mix and match them in any combination to see how they will look together in a design. If you want to create this library of patterns for yourself, you'll need to knit generously-sized gauge swatches.

Once you've collected a group of patterns you think are compatible, it's time to make one large swatch which includes all the patterns, even if you've swatched each pattern individually. Often the background stitches separating the cable patterns will make the patterns stand out or recede—an effect you can fully appreciate only in a larger swatch. Also, you may decide that the cables could benefit from being separated by a small 2-stitch cable or column of twisted knit stitches. It may be that one of the cables "fights" with its neighbors, in which case you will have to consider discarding it in favor of another pattern, or moving it to a different location in the design.

Knit a swatch containing the center panel and the cables and filler stitches to one side of it. Knitting this large a swatch takes time and yarn, yes, but it allows you to see just what the patterns will look like when knitted next to each other. And you will use it in the next step where you will need to have an accurate measurement of the widths of each of the cable patterns.

I assure you that making this swatch is not a waste of time. But if you would like to have a finished piece to show for your time, you can use Elizabeth Zimmermann's method and knit a swatch of the design as it will appear on the front of the garment. The width of the front of a sweater is about the same as the circumference of an adult head, and you can turn your swatch into a matching hat for your sweater.

6.2 Choosing a Garment Style

For years I thought that the only suitable garment style for an Aran was the dropped-shoulder style. I began knitting during the period of time when dropped-shoulder styles were very popular. It *is* easier to knit them and easier to write and size patterns for them. Because a dropped-shoulder Aran is made mostly of rectangular shapes, vertical cable patterns fit easily onto the body plan. Less shaping allows the patterning to be the focus of attention. Dropped-shoulder styles also have the advantage of being constructed without complicated seams.

However, lots of people—myself included—don't look good in dropped-shoulder garments, or find them too casual-looking for their needs. Don't limit yourself to dropped-shoulder styles because they seem easy. If you can work garment shaping in Stockinette Stitch, you can work garment shaping in Seed or Moss Stitch, too. Other garment styles are no more complicated than dropped-shoulder styles if you think of them as rectangles with additional stitches surrounding them in which all the shaping takes place.

I encourage you to look at your wardrobe and assess what kinds of garments you already have that fit you well. Become familiar with those styles that flatter your body and don't try to wear something unflattering just because it's currently fashionable.

Appendix B contains a worksheet for you to use when planning a sweater. It provides guidance on taking your body measurements (or those of the intended wearer) and a place to write them down. Make copies of this worksheet, and use a different one for each of your projects.

6.3 Coordinating the Garment

Once you've selected your cable patterns, swatched them, and made a decision about the garment style and direction of knitting, it's time to put it all together. The body, ribbing, and sleeves all need to coordinate with each other for a coherent design.

6.3.1 The Body

Before I started using my charting software, I used to plan the body of my design by taking a piece of graph paper (I used big sheets from the local blueprint store) and drawing a line across it near the bottom. Starting at the right side of the paper, I counted as many squares as I had filler stitches on one side, then drew a vertical line. Next, I put in the number of background stitches between the filler stitches and the first cable or divider pattern, then the cable or divider pattern itself. I continued in this way, moving from right to left, using one square to symbolize each stitch and making vertical lines to show the division between each element.

I also wrote the name of the cable pattern above or below its position on the line, as well as its width. When I finished, I checked to see that I included *all* the elements—it's very easy to leave out background stitches or spacer patterns. I then added together the widths of all the patterns to see if they matched the desired width of the sweater. At that point, I made adjustments by adding or removing background stitches, adding or removing filler stitches, or both. Occasionally I needed to eliminate, add, or change some of the cable patterns.

After I had determined that I had a good arrangement of cables, background stitches, and filler stitches, I counted the number of squares to determine the number of body stitches required. All that remained was to write down the row-by-row instructions for each cable.

Now that I have charting software, this planning process proceeds much quicker. I have a fairly comprehensive library of charted cable patterns stored in my computer. I simply print out the chart for each cable in my design (each chart includes the cable pattern and a single purl stitch to either side of it), then cut them apart and paste them onto a large sheet of paper. I then have a detailed stitch-by-stitch picture of my design. I can draw in any shaping considerations (such as neck openings) on my chart using colored pencils.

If you choose to use charts in this way, keep these points in mind:

• Make sure that the cable patterns all begin on the same row; even within the same stitch dictionary, some cable pattern directions begin on wrong-side rows and some on right-side rows. Choose one and adjust the other stitch patterns up or down one row as necessary.

• The cable patterns should be "mirror-imaged" on either side of the center panel. For a pattern which moves from left to right and back again, such as a zig-zag cable, start the pattern on row 1 on one side of the center panel, and start with the center row of the pattern repeat on the other side of the center panel. For rope cables, plan for right crosses on one side of the garment and left crosses on the other side.

6.3.2 The Trim

Ribbing is the trim most often found on sweaters. It holds the fabric snug against the waistline and wrists, and provides a simple frame for the patterning on the rest of the garment. If you choose to have ribbing, keep in mind that because there are many more body stitches in an Aran sweater than in a plain stockinette stitch sweater of the same size, the standard formula of "total body stitches minus 10-20%" for ribbing might not work—your ribbing might not be tight enough. Instead, use about 30% fewer stitches for the ribbing. You may need to adjust that number even further if you've selected a ribbing pattern which doesn't have a lot of elasticity, or to minimize cable splay. As always, swatching the ribbing pattern at the base of your cable combination swatch will help you make that determination.

Note, however, that ribbing isn't a required element of an Aran design. Other options include:

• A skirt at the bottom of your garment instead of a regular ribbing pattern
• Welts
• No trim at all

6.3.3 The Sleeves

Aran sweaters usually have a cable pattern running down the center of the sleeve that is the same as or similar to one of the patterns used in the body. A narrow pattern 2-3" wide works well, especially if it will be carried up onto the saddle. This pattern is flanked on either side by filler stitches, in which the sleeve shaping takes place.

It's possible to have cable patterning all over the sleeve, although it is trickier to shape. If you choose this option and are knitting your sleeves from the shoulder to the cuff, be sure to pick up additional stitches around the armhole opening (more than the usual "3 stitches for every 4 rows") to compensate for the tendency of the cable patterns to draw in.

A good way to determine sleeve length is by measuring the wingspan of the intended wearer. Have the person stand with their arms outstretched and slightly bent.

Measure the distance from wrist to wrist across the back. Subtract the width at chest measurement from this number and divide the result in half to determine the length of each sleeve.

If making an Aran sweater for a child younger than about age 10, you don't need to do any sleeve shaping; simply knit a long tube from shoulder to wrist. Their arms are generally pretty chubby. The decreases normally made along the length of an adult sleeve can all be made in the row or round just above the ribbing.

6.3.3.1 Dropped-Shoulder and Peasant Sleeves

Designer Joan Schrouder discovered that when the shaping is placed to either side of a central cable pattern running along the top of a sleeve, it changes the shape of the sleeve to a more anatomically correct and better-fitting one (Figure 57). This method also makes the increases or decreases less noticeable than they would be if placed along a seam at the bottom of the sleeve. Using Joan's method, the shaping does not interrupt the filler pattern surrounding the cable pattern.

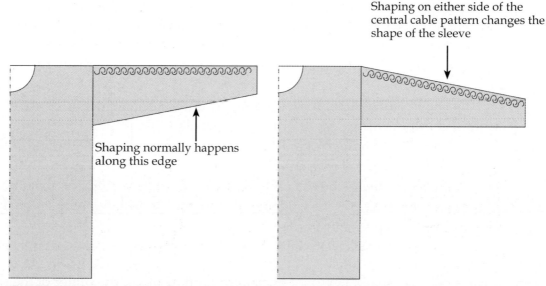

Shaping on either side of the central cable pattern changes the shape of the sleeve

Shaping normally happens along this edge

Fig. 57. *Placing the shaping along either side of the cable patterning of a sleeve changes the shape of the sleeve.*

6.3.3.2 Set-in Sleeves

Please don't shy away from making Arans with set-in sleeves because set-in sleeves are considered "difficult." They can be tricky, but the fit is often so superior to the other sleeve styles that the extra work is worth it. If you are new to set-in sleeves, try the shallow set-in sleeve first.

Standard Cap. Knitters often avoid designing sweaters with set-in sleeves because they dislike having to figure out the sleeve cap shaping. Let's use the following example to illustrate how to figure out the cap shaping for a standard sleeve cap. (Deborah Newton's *Designing Knitwear* has a very thorough explanation of sleeve cap shaping.)

Suppose we are making an Aran with set-in sleeves and we know that our gauge over Moss Stitch—the filler stitch—is 5 stitches and 7 rows to the inch. This design has a cable pattern centered on the sleeve, and it is 2½" wide.

The depth of the armhole is 7¾". Therefore, the width at the top of the sleeve—before the cap shaping begins—should be approximately twice that depth, or 15½".

Armed with this information, we make the following calculations:

15½" minus 2½" equals 13", or 6½" of filler stitches on either side of center cable

6½" x 5 sts/in = 32½ filler stitches (round to 33) on either side of the center cable

We can forget about those cable stitches at the center of the sleeve for a moment. If the set-in sleeve has a saddle, the cable will be continued up into the saddle. If the sleeve doesn't have a saddle, these stitches will be bound off to form the top of the cap. What is important to the cap shaping are those filler stitches at either side.

The height of the cap needs to be about ⅔ of the armhole depth, or about 5¼". Multipled by our row gauge of 7 rows/in, that allows 36 rows for the cap shaping.

Begin the cap shaping by binding off a set of stitches at the beginning of the first two rows. The number of stitches to be bound off should be about the same as the number of stitches bound off to begin the armhole shaping on the body. For purposes of this example, we will bind off 5 stitches at the beginning of the first two rows of the cap shaping.

This leaves 34 rows over which to decrease 56 stitches (we have 66 stitches available for the cap shaping and we've already bound off 10 of them). Because we want the top of the cap to have a flat shape, we're going to bind off 2" worth (12 stitches) over the last ½" (or about 4 rows) in the sleeve cap. That leaves us with 44 stitches (22 on each side) that need to be eliminated over 30 rows.

Note that 22 doesn't divide evenly into 30, and that's okay. The rate of decreasing isn't even—the cap shaping starts with a 45° angle followed by a flatter angle of about 30°. Begin by decreasing one stitch at either end of every right-side row 9 times (that uses up 18 of the 30 rows), then decrease one stitch at either end of every row 12 times (that uses up the remaining 12 of the 30 rows). The math wizzes among you will notice that only 21 stitches have been decreased on either side, not 22. The math doesn't always work out perfectly. Sometimes it's necessary to fudge; in this case, add another decrease row (for a total of 31) before working the final cap shaping. The final cap shaping involves binding off those last 12 stitches—3 stitches at the beginning of the next 4 rows—then binding off the unshaped stitches at the top of the cap, or continuing on with them to create a saddle.

Remember that the measurement along the curved edge of the sleeve cap should be equal to the measurement along the edge of the armhole. If there are any doubts, measure the edge of the armhole opening and compare it to the measurement along the curved edge of the sleeve cap. This can be done by drawing the outline of the sleeve cap and the armhole on a piece of graph paper which has the same gauge as the knitting, or by using a flexible ruler. If the two measurements are roughly the same, the sleeve will fit nicely into the armhole (any excess should occur in the sleeve cap—it can be eased into the armhole opening).

Shallow Cap. This sleeve style is combined with a slightly more oversized body and deeper armhole than a regular set-in sleeve garment, which gives it more of a casual look.

Begin the cap shaping as for a standard set-in sleeve, by binding off the same number of stitches as at the beginning of the armhole shaping on the body. Decrease one stitch at both ends of every right-side row until the height of the cap is about 1-3". At that point, bind off groups of 2 or 3 stitches over the next 1" worth of rows. Then if the design has a saddle, bind off all but the saddle stitches and knit the saddle to the desired length. Otherwise, bind off all stitches.

6.3.4 The Saddles

The presence or absence of a saddle in an Aran design is a topic of much debate, particularly among purists who believe that any "traditional" Aran *should* include saddles. On the other hand, some people think that saddles make them look like football players. Consider the overall design and the intended wearer.

Not all cable patterns work equally well as saddle cables. When choosing a cable to place on the saddle of an Aran, select ones 2-3" wide (cables wider than 2-3" are best used on T-sleeve or wide-saddle Arans). In order to make it more likely that the cable ends at a visually pleasing spot at the cuff, the row repeat of the cable should be 24 rows or fewer. Avoid delicate or feathery cables, unless the theme of the design calls for those kinds of stitch patterns.

Note that the presence or absence of saddles affects the neck shaping. A saddle provides "drop" to the neckline; that "drop," or depth, depends upon the width of the saddle. A narrow saddle creates a higher neckline, while a wider saddle creates a lower one. A completely unshaped neckline—with the drop being provided by the saddles only—will be square.

The presence of saddles also affects the armhole depth. A saddle contributes half its width to the total armhole depth; take note of this and adjust the armhole depth of the body accordingly.

Many Aran saddles have a single cable panel running down the center (see Figure 58, top). On either side of this panel are two purl stitches. I'm not fond of this look for a couple of reasons. First, it's difficult to pick up stitches neatly along those purled edges. Second, the cable looks as though it's "floating," or not really anchored to the rest of the design.

I much prefer the saddle style shown on the bottom in Figure 58. This saddle has a center cable, but also two narrower cables to either side. The narrow cables on either side of the saddle can easily be replaced by a single column of knit stitches (twisted knit stitches look especially nice here). When combined with a stockinette stitch selvedge for picking up stitches (see Section 6.3.4.2), those narrow cables or line of knit stitches help to anchor the saddles to the rest of the design.

Joining the saddle and body pieces can be done in one of several ways. Each option has advantages and disadvantages. The options are outlined below.

Fig 58. *A saddle with no edge stitches (top) and with edge stitches (bottom).*

6.3.4.1 Perpendicular Join

This kind of join allows the saddle to be knitted and joined to a bottom-up body in one step, eliminating any sewing. In order to use this method, the body stitches must be left "live" and not bound off. (If decreases are required to eliminate cable splay, work them on the last pattern row.)

A perpendicular join worked in plain Stockinette fabric calls for the body stitches to be joined to the saddle stitches on every other row. However, an Aran sweater usually has more stitches per inch of pattern than in a sweater knit in plain Stockinette Stitch. If joined every other row, the top of the body tends to spread unattractively along the saddle; therefore, the body stitches should be joined to the saddle on every row.

Step 1. Work the body pieces to the desired armhole depth minus half the width of the saddle, incorporating neck shaping if desired.

Step 2. Place the stitches on either side of the neck opening onto separate double-pointed needles. Prepare to knit across the right side of a saddle.

Step 3. Working only on the stitches of the saddle, knit across to the last saddle stitch, place a body stitch from the double-pointed needle onto the needle holding the saddle stitches, and work an SSK on these two stitches. Turn work.

Step 4. Slip the next body stitch from the double-pointed needle to the working needle, and purl those two stitches together through the back of the loops. Work across to the last saddle stitch. Slip the next body stitch from the double-pointed needle to the needle holding the saddle needle and purl those two stitches together. Turn work.

Step 5. Slip the next body stitch from the double-pointed needle to the needle holding the saddle stitches and knit this stitch together with the first saddle stitch.

Repeat from Step 3 until all stitches of front and back have been joined to the saddle. Place the saddle stitches on a holder to be picked up later for the neckband.

Note that this technique works in either direction: if working the sleeve from the cuff to the shoulder, continue on the saddle stitches only once the sleeve is complete, joining them to the body as work progresses toward the neck edge. Alternatively, begin at the neck edge, knitting and joining the saddle to the body. Once the saddle is complete, pick up and knit the stitches for the sleeve around the armhole opening.

6.3.4.2 Sewing In
Saddles can be sewn into the body of the sweater, just as any two pieces of knitted fabric can be seamed. This method allows for the possibility of later repair, should the saddles area of a sweater become ripped or worn.

6.3.4.3 Picking Up Along Saddle Edges and Knitting Down
When setting up your saddle pattern for this option, add a selvedge stitch to either edge. This selvedge stitch is worked as a knit stitch on all right-side rows and as a purl stitch on all wrong-side rows, creating a Stockinette selvedge. Such a selvedge provides a stable edge in which to pick up the front and back body stitches, when knitting from the top down.

Useful Aran Knitting Tips

Years of designing and knitting Arans have given me a whole arsenal of tips and tricks to make the job go easier. Here are some of my favorites.

7.1 Moving Stitches

Like many aspects of knitting, each knitter has a preferred method of moving stitches.

7.1.1 Cable Needles

Figure 59 shows some of the most popular cable needle shapes and sizes. Thin aluminum-coated glove needles (about 4" long) work well. Novice cablers may prefer to use one of the shaped ones as the stitches are less likely to fall off the needle. The wooden ones are good to use when working with a slippery yarn like a slick cotton or rayon.

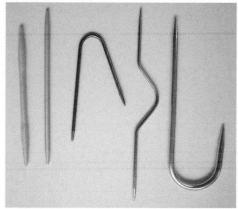

Fig. 59: *A variety of cable needles. From L to R: Straight wooden, straight aluminum-coated, U-shaped, gull-wing shaped, and J-shaped.*

7.1.2 Cabling Without a Needle

Many knitters learn to cable without a needle, which increases knitting speed and eliminates an extra tool.

Shown here is a 3-stitch-over-3-stitch left cross made without a cable needle.

Step 1. *Take the RH needle behind the LH needle and insert it into the 4th, 5th and 6th stitches on the LH needle.*

Step 2. *Slip those stitches to the RH needle, causing the 1st, 2nd, and 3rd stitches to fall to the front.*

Step 3. *Insert the LH needle into the free stitches.*

Step 4. *Slip the stitches from the RH needle back to the LH needle — now all the stitches are in position for the cable.*

Step 5. *Knit across the stitches and complete the cable.*

7.2 Marking the Work

Although it's good to learn to "read" your knitting, visual aids such as stitch and row markers can help keep track of shaping.

7.2.1 Stitch Markers

These are extremely useful for separating the individual patterns in the body of your knitting. Get a variety of sizes and colors. The rubber O-ring kind are especially nice because they don't fly off the needles as easily as the plastic kind. These can often be found in bulk at hardware stores.

7.2.2 Row Markers

I use safety pins as row markers. I have a wide assortment of silver- and gold-colored ones in different sizes. Small ones mark decreases along sleeves, larger ones mark front and back pieces.

7.2.3 Hang Tags

One of my students came up with this great idea for keeping her place in a pattern. She wrote the directions for each cable pattern on a large hang tag (available at office supply stores) and safety-pinned the tag to the base of each cable panel. As she worked across the row, if she needed to refer to the pattern for a panel, she simply looked at the hang tag. For patterns with large row repeats, a hang tag might not be big enough, in which case a 3x5" index card could be used.

7.3 Better Bobbles

Knitters sometimes avoid including cables with bobbles in their designs because they think the bobbles look sloppy. Here are a few tips to make the bobbles on your next project look terrific.

7.3.1 Tip #1: Use Yarn Overs

Most bobble instructions specify to make three, five, or more stitches from one by knitting alternately into the front and back of a single stitch. These increases tend to distort and stretch the base stitch. A better method, which gives the same number of increases, is to use yarn overs for some of the increases. To make five stitches from one, for example, work [k1, yo, k1, yo, k1] into the base stitch.

7.3.2 Tip #2: Pair the Decreases

Most bobble instructions specify that the knitter should increase stitches, work two, four, or more rows on just the increased bobble stitches, then decrease by passing the 2nd, 3rd, 4th, and 5th stitches of the bobble over the first one. The problem with this method is that it makes a bobble which insists on listing to one side.

A much rounder bobble that sits perfectly straight on the fabric can be made as follows:

Row 1: Work [k1, yo, k1, yo, k1] into the next stitch. Turn.

Row 2: Purl. Turn.
Row 3: K2tog, k1, SSK. Turn.
Row 4: Purl. Turn.
Row 5: Slip 2 — k1 — p2sso.

Note that in row 3, two of the five bobble stitches are decreased by working a k2tog and a SSK, which are paired on either side of the bobble. On row 5, the remaining two extra bobble stitches are decreased by working a center double decrease. Because all of these decreases are symmetrical, the result is a lovely round bobble that does not lean to one side.

7.3.3 Tip #3: Strangle the Bobble

Even bobbles made according to the instructions given above sometimes want to hide on the wrong side of the work. When you've finished the bobble, "strangle" it on the next wrong-side row by purling into the back of the stitch to twist it. Doing so will help keep the bobble from falling to the wrong side of the work.

7.3.4 Tip #4: Learn to Knit Back Backwards

Working bobbles on a large piece of heavily textured knitting can become tedious, and flipping the piece of knitting from one side to the other stresses the fabric. Alleviate the problem by learning to "knit back backwards," or knit from left to right with the right side of the fabric facing you. *Meg Swansen's Knitting* has an excellent explanation and illustration of this technique.

7.4 Decreasing Into Cables

Garment shaping in areas of cable patterning can be a real challenge. Done correctly, this shaping adds to the overall look of the garment. Done sloppily, it can ruin an otherwise beautiful piece of knitting.

Sometimes a pattern calls for a decrease in the same place as a cable crossing. If there aren't enough stitches to do a complete cross, it's tempting to continue on in plain stockinette. However, nothing looks worse than a place on a sweater where there ought to be a cable crossing and there isn't. In this situation, preserve the cable crossing if at all possible. It's possible to cross a cable even without the requisite number of stitches. For instance, if the pattern calls for a 3-over-3 stitch cross but there are only five stitches, make a 3-over-2 cross and no one will be the wiser.

Another place where it's often necessary to decrease a cable is in a bind-off row, as for a neck opening. Decreasing while simultaneously binding off stitches helps alleviate cable splay along this edge (see Chapter 5 for more on cable splay).

7.5 Easier Finishing

I've always maintained that good finishing of a garment depends a lot on what you do while you're knitting it. Here are some places to which you need to pay particular attention.

7.5.1 Filler Stitches

The filler stitches on either side of the body pieces can present a real seaming challenge when the pieces are knit flat. My favorite seaming method is mattress stitch, which works best when the first and last stitch on each right-side row is a knit, and the first and last stitch on each wrong-side row is a purl. Unfortunately, many knit-purl stitch combinations used as filler stitches do not incorporate such an edge. It has to be factored in when determining how many stitches to cast on. Doing so will greatly add to the ease of seaming the pieces together.

7.5.2 Armhole Edges

Another important edge is along the armhole opening. If the stockinette selvedge described above has been factored in during the knitting of the front and back body pieces, it's not an issue. However, when the body has been knit in the round and split at the beginning of the armhole, I like to cast on an additional stitch at the beginning of the first two rows of the upper body pieces. These cast-on stitches are worked as a stockinette stitch selvedge. When it's time to pick up the stitches for the sleeves and knit down to the cuff, that selvedge provides a stable edge for the sleeve and prevents the sleeve from interfering with the patterning on the body.

Fig. 60: *A mis-crossed cable.*

7.6 Fixing Mistakes

It's a terrible feeling to get halfway up the body of a sweater and realize that there is a mistake 3" back. Get into the habit of checking your work—I like to think of it as *admiring* the work—every couple of inches or so. That way, if a mistake needs to be fixed, it'll be less complicated to do so.

Don't panic if a mistake in the cabling makes itself known. Check to see if it's possible to fix just that cable.

Shown in Figure 60 is a swatch with a mis-crossed cable. The cable in the middle should have a 3-stitch-over-3-stitch right cross to match the other cables in the swatch. Instead, the cable has a 3-stitch-over-3-stitch *left* cross.

The following photos illustrate the steps involved in fixing a mis-crossed cable.

Step 1. *Remove the working needle from the stitches.*

Step 2. *Ladder down the cable, carefully pulling the yarn out of the stitches.*

Step 3. *Place the loose stitches onto a cable needle or other holder.*

Step 4. *Correctly reknit the stitches on the holder using the strands of yarn that were pulled out. Be careful to reknit the stitches with the strands from the proper rows.*

I've used this method with great success when I wanted to completely change a pattern in a design. About 2" into one of my designs I decided that one of the cable patterns was fighting with the rest of the patterns. I took it down to the ribbing and reknit another pattern with the same stitch count in its place.

7.7 Tubular Cast-On For Neckband

Use a tubular cast-on when beginning a top-down Aran by knitting the neckband first. This kind of cast-on gives an extremely flexible edge, especially suitable for turtleneck sweaters.

There are a variety of ways to cast on for a tubularly-knit ribbing. Some use the working yarn, some use waste yarn. For an overview of the different methods, see Charlotte Morris's articles "Taming the Tubular Cast-On," Parts 1 and 2, in *Knitter's Magazine* Nos. 63 and 64, Summer 2001 and Fall 2001.

My favorite method involves a provisional (or temporary) cast-on using waste yarn and a crocheted chain.

Step 1. Using a length of waste yarn, crochet a chain a few links longer than half the number of stitches needed for the neckband.

Step 2. For this step, use a needle several times smaller than the one you plan to use to knit the ribbing. (If you use the same size needle as for the rest of the ribbing, this cast-on edge will flare unattractively.) Beginning at one end and using the garment yarn, *pick up one stitch in the "bump" on the back of the chain, then make a yarn over. Repeat from *, until you have picked one more than the necessary number of stitches (ending with a picked-up stitch).

Step 3. Join, being careful not to twist. On this first round, slip the picked-up stitches as if to purl, with yarn in back, and purl the yarn-overs. Knit the last stitch and the first stitch of the round together.

Step 4. On the second round, slip the stitches which were worked on the previous round as if to purl, with yarn in front, and knit the stitches which were slipped.

Step 5. On the third and all subsequent rounds, change to needles of the size specified for the ribbing. Knit the knit stitches and purl the purl stitches, as for regular k1, p1 ribbing.

Part Two

From Concept to Sweater

Constructing an Aran

8

The number of ways to knit an Aran sweater are staggering. Choices include various sleeve/body joins, knitting from the bottom up or the top down, and flat versus in-the-round knitting.

Each of Chapters 9 through 15 examines a particular sleeve/body join; this chapter handles issues common to some of them. It guides you through the initial steps of constructing an Aran, then directs you to the appropriate section of a following chapter, depending on your choice of sleeve.

The first choice you need to make is whether to knit from the bottom up or the top-down. Next, you'll need to decide if you prefer to knit flat pieces or work the garment in the round. Finally, factor in the kind of sleeve style you want for the garment—dropped-shoulder, peasant-sleeve, or set-in sleeve. If you wish to make a raglan Aran sweater, an Aran vest, a T-sleeve style Aran, or an Aran with a wide yoke, skip to Chapter 12, 13, 14, or 15.

As a designer, I don't advocate any of these methods over the other, although I do admit to a personal preference for top-down knitting. I like the flexibility of choosing a construction method uniquely suited to each project. A tailored Aran might best be knit in pieces, with close attention paid to the shaping and finishing details. A more casual Aran might be easiest to knit from the top down. Factor the needs of your project into your choice.

8.1 Bottom-Up Construction

These are the methods most familiar to the majority of knitters. After all, knitting creates a vertical piece of fabric, beginning at the bottom and working toward the top.

Knitters debate the merits of knitting flat pieces of fabric which are later seamed together versus knitting a one-piece tube of fabric. Each approach has advantages and disadvantages. Which you use depends on the needs of the design and your personal preference.

8.1.1 Knitting Bottom-up Flat Pieces

This approach treats knitted fabric much like woven fabric: The knitter makes and shapes pieces of fabric which are later sewn together. The individual pieces of knitting are smaller and much more portable, without the weight of an entire garment hanging from the needles. Shaping (*e.g.*, at the waist or bust) is often easier to manage within each piece. Seams can provide stability to a heavily textured garment, preventing it from stretching out of shape.

The main drawback to knitting an Aran in pieces is that the pieces must be sewn together. Many knitters lack the confidence and skills to do this neatly. Careful attention is needed while knitting the individual pieces to ensure that they can be assembled with a professional look.

Step 1. Cast on for the ribbing or skirt. Work to the desired depth.

   The number of stitches cast on for the ribbing depends upon how much the bottom of the garment needs to draw in. Determine the number of stitches needed for the body width measurement first, then subtract a percentage of that number to determine how many stitches to cast on for the ribbing. Using 10% fewer stitches will give a ribbing that does not draw in or cling very much. Using 30% fewer stitches will give a very tight, clinging ribbing.

Step 2. Make any necessary increases and establish the body pattern.

Step 3. Work until the back measures the desired length to underarm.

   For a dropped-shoulder Aran with saddles, go to section 9.1.1.
   For a dropped-shoulder Aran without saddles, go to section 9.2.1.
   For a peasant-sleeve Aran with saddles, go to section 10.1.1.
   For a peasant-sleeve Aran without saddles, go to section 10.2.1.
   For a set-in sleeve Aran with saddles, go to section 11.1.1.
   For a set-in sleeve Aran without saddles, go to section 11.2.1.

8.1.2 Knitting Bottom-up in the Round

Knitting in the round is an alternative construction method which avoids many of the pitfalls of knitting Arans in pieces and seaming. Besides, the Aran evolved from a garment which was knit in the round—for very good reasons. A Scottish fisher gansey knit in the round had no seamlines to split open. Sleeves were picked up along the edge of the body and knit down, allowing them to be repaired later when cuffs frayed.

However, Arans are much heavier garments than the fisher ganseys from which they evolved. All that weight hanging off the knitting needles can be difficult for some knitters to manage. A garment constructed in this way is not very portable. Some knitters also feel that these kinds of garments have a greater tendency to stretch out of shape.

One style which does lend itself well to being knit in the round from the bottom up is the raglan Aran (see Chapter 12). Knitting a raglan Aran this way allows for use of one of the percentage methods of designing (see *Knitting Without Tears* or *The Sweater*

Workshop for detailed instructions on knitting raglan sweaters using the percentage method).

Step 1. Cast on for the ribbing or skirt. Work to the desired depth.

   The number of stitches cast on for the ribbing depends upon how much the bottom of the garment needs to draw in. Determine the number of stitches needed for twice the body width measurement first, then subtract a percentage of that number to determine how many stitches to cast on for the ribbing. Using 10% fewer stitches will give a ribbing that does not draw in or cling very much. Using 30% fewer stitches will give a very tight, clinging ribbing.

Step 2. Make any necessary increases and establish the body pattern. Place markers to denote the beginning of the round and the halfway point of the round.

Step 3. Work until the body measures the desired length to underarm.

   For a dropped-shoulder Aran with saddles, go to section 9.1.2.
   For a dropped-shoulder Aran without saddles, go to section 9.2.2.
   For a peasant-sleeve Aran with saddles, go to section 10.1.2.
   For a peasant-sleeve Aran without saddles, go to section 10.2.2.

8.2 Top-Down Construction

I have solid reasons for preferring top-down construction for most of my Arans. They include these:

• It's most important in an Aran design to have the center panel cable pattern appear in a visually pleasing way just below the wearer's face (*e.g.*, a cable repeat, not a cable which stops at an awkward place in the repeat). Making this happen when knitting from the bottom to the top takes a fair bit of advance planning. Making this happen when knitting from the top down is much easier — simply begin the cable below the neck opening at a suitable point in the pattern repeat.

• Designs knit from the bottom up usually begin with the ribbing (unless a provisional cast-on is used). It's often easier to decide on a suitable ribbing or trim once the entire sweater has been knit.

• Making the design "flow" from the cables into the ribbing is often easier when knitting from the top down.

• Knitting from the top allows for adjustments to the length of the body or sleeves if it appears that yarn amounts are running short.

I've knit many Arans from the top down over the years. I've tried virtually every method available. This section presents those top-down versions which I think are most visually interesting and require only moderate designing skills. Where appropriate, I provide references to books, designs, and articles which cover some of the more challenging top-down designs.

Here, I've divided top-down construction into two parts: 1) top-down construction in which the *neckband* is knitted first, and 2) top-down construction in which the *body* is knitted first. The instructions cover the knitting of each style to the base of the armhole openings. At that point, please refer to the chapter on each sleeve style for instructions on completing the garment.

If you're interested in exploring top-down knitting in greater detail, the best reference I can suggest is Barbara Walker's *Knitting From the Top*. This reference book belongs on every designer's bookshelf.

8.2.1 Neckband-First

This method is one I've seen touted as the "true" method for knitting a traditional Aran sweater. While I doubt that assertion, it remains a legitimate method of beginning an Aran sweater. It's a bit trickier than the other top-down methods, because it requires familiarity with working short rows within Aran patterns.

This section provides an overview of the neckband-first method. For in-depth exploration, I highly recommend Dixie Falls' book *Aran From the Neck Down*. Joan Schrouder designed a lovely Aran using Dixie's technique which was first published in *Knitter's Magazine* No. 16. Although that issue has long been out of print, Joan's design is still available in the book *The Best of Knitter's: Arans & Celtics*.

Steps 1-4 are the same for both unshaped and shaped neckline openings.

Step 1. Cast on a sufficient number of stitches for the neckband (for an adult sweater in a worsted weight yarn, this number is somewhere between 90 and 100 stitches, depending upon the yarn and the intended recipient). An elastic cast-on method is essential for a good fit. I highly recommend the tubular cast-on, directions for which are given in Chapter 7.

Step 2. Knit the neckband to the desired depth. Divide the stitches into thirds: Place one-third on a holder for the front, one-third on a holder for the back, and divide the remaining one-third in half for the saddles (Figure 61). This division

Place these stitches on a holder for the back

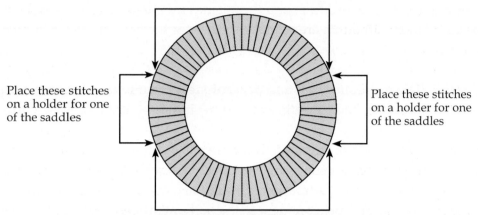

Place these stitches on a holder for one of the saddles

Place these stitches on a holder for one of the saddles

Place these stitches on a holder for the front

Fig. 61: *Dividing the stitches of the neckband.*

does not have to be exact. Depending on the layout of the cable patterns, stitches can be added to or subtracted from each of the sections as necessary.

Step 3. Place the stitches for one of the saddles onto a working needle and knit it to the desired length.

The saddle length is determined by the sleeve style: For a dropped-shoulder sweater, subtract the width of the neck opening from the body width measurement, then divide that number in half to determine the saddle length. For peasant- and set-in sleeve styles, subtract the width of the neck opening from the cross-shoulder measurement, then divide that number in half to determine the saddle length.

End having knit a wrong-side row and place the stitches on a holder. Repeat for the second saddle.

2. Knit the back neck stitches from their holder.

3. Pick up stitches along this saddle edge.

1. Pick up stitches along this saddle edge.

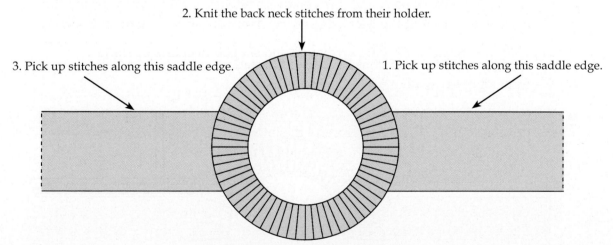

Fig. 62: *Picking up stitches for the back.*

Step 4. Working from right to left (Figure 62), pick up stitches for the back along the edge of the first saddle, knit the stitches for the back neck from the neckband holder, then pick up the remaining stitches for the back along the edge of the other saddle.

Step 5 (Dropped-shoulder and peasant-sleeve versions). Continue on all stitches to the desired armhole depth, and end having worked a wrong-side row.

Step 5 (Set-in sleeve version). Continue on all stitches to a point a few inches short of the desired armhole depth. Here, begin making increases (one stitch at each end of every other row) to add approximately half of the extra fabric needed to widen the cross-shoulder measurement to the body width measurement. When to begin adding these extra stitches depends on the difference between the cross-shoulder measurement and the body width measurement. If the difference between these two measurements is small (2-4"), begin increasing just a few inches short of the base of the armhole. If the difference is larger (5-8"), begin increasing farther from the base of the armhole. The remaining width needed will be cast on altogether at the base of the armhole opening.

Step 6. *Decision point:* Knit an *unshaped* (Option 1) or *shaped* (Option 2) front neckline.

> Option 1. For an *unshaped* front neckline, repeat steps 4 and 5 for the front of the garment. Work to the same pattern row as the back and place the stitches on a holder. Continue with Step 9.

> Option 2. For a *shaped* front neckline, pick up stitches along the edge of one saddle only. Work back and forth on these stitches, adding a stitch from the neckband holder at the neck edge every other row and working a short row wrap to avoid a hole (Figure 63). Continue in this manner until approximately ¼ of the front neck stitches have been worked from the holder. Place the right front stitches on a holder.

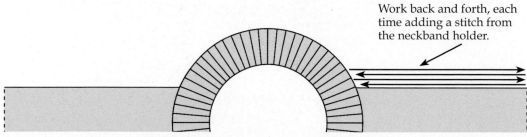

Work back and forth, each time adding a stitch from the neckband holder.

Fig. 63: *Working short rows on the right front.*

Step 7. Pick up stitches for the left front along the edge of the other saddle. Work back and forth on these stitches, adding a stitch from the neckband holder at the neck edge every other row and working a short row wrap to avoid a hole. Continue in this manner until approximately ¼ of the front neck stitches have been worked from the holder and the left and right fronts are on the same pattern row.

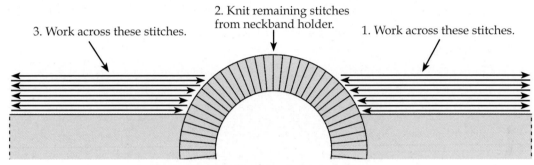

Fig. 64: *Completed short rows.*

Step 8. Reattach yarn to the right front stitches and work across. Knit the remaining stitches from the neckband holder, then knit across the stitches of the left front (Figure 64). Work the front to match the back, and end having worked a wrong-side row.

Step 9. Continue as appropriate for your chosen sleeve style.

For a dropped-shoulder Aran with saddles, go to section 9.1.3.
For a peasant-sleeve Aran with saddles, go to to section 10.1.3.
For a set-in sleeve Aran with saddles, go to to section 11.1.2.

8.2.2 Body First

Which of the first two of these body-first methods you choose depends on whether or not your Aran design includes saddles.

8.2.2.1 Top-Down Arans With Saddles

Knitting top-down Arans with saddles is a bit easier than knitting them without saddles, as the saddles provide drop to the front and back necklines, and also edges along which to pick up stitches for the front and back.

Step 1. Cast on enough stitches to accommodate a cable pattern and selvedge stitches.

Step 2. Work the saddle to the desired length (Figure 65). This length is determined by subtracting the width of the neck opening from the total body width measurement (for a dropped-shoulder version) or the cross-shoulder measurement (for a peasant- or set-in sleeve version). Divide the result in half to determine the length of each saddle. For example, if the body width is 22" and the neck opening is 8", the saddles each will be 7" long. End having knit a wrong-side row and place the stitches on a holder. Repeat for the second saddle.

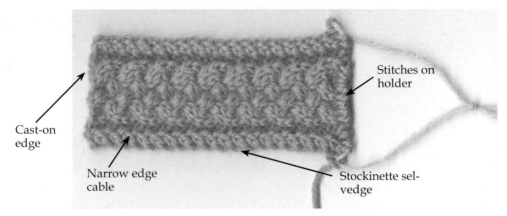

Cast-on edge

Stitches on holder

Narrow edge cable

Stockinette sel- vedge

Fig. 65: *A saddle completed as far as the shoulder.*

Step 3. Pick up stitches along the edge of one saddle (Figure 66), making sure that it is oriented so that the stitches on the holder are at the outside edge, later to be picked up and worked as part of the sleeve.

Fig. 66: *Picking up stitches along the edge of one of the saddles.*

Step 4. Cast on additional stitches for the neck opening (I prefer a cable cast-on or knitted cast-on), and pick up the remaining stitches along the edge of the second saddle (Figure 67).

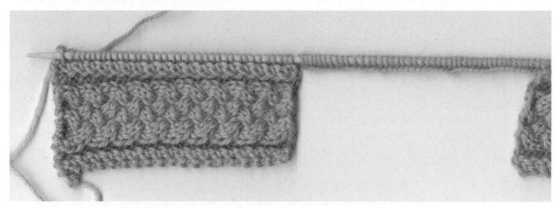

Fig. 67: *Stitches for the back neck have been cast on, and the remaining stitches are picked up along the edge of the second saddle.*

It's also possible you will need to pick up more stitches than you can pick up from the saddle. If that happens, increase to the correct number of upper body stitches on the first row of the body.

Step 5 (Dropped-shoulder and peasant-sleeve versions). Establish the body pattern and work to the desired armhole depth. End having worked a wrong-side row and place those stitches on a holder.

Step 5 (Set-in sleeve version). Establish the body pattern and continue on all stitches to a point a few inches short of the desired armhole depth. Here, begin making increases (one stitch at each end of every other row) to add approximately half of the extra fabric needed to widen the cross-shoulder measurement to the body width measurement. When to begin adding these extra stitches depends on the difference between the cross-shoulder measurement and the body width measurement. If the difference between these two measurements is small (2-4"), begin increasing just a few inches short of the base of the armhole. If the difference is larger (5-8"), begin increasing farther from the base of the armhole. The remaining width needed will be cast on altogether at the base of the armhole opening.

Step 6. *Decision point:* Knit an unshaped (Option 1) or shaped (Option 2) front neckline.

Option 1. For an *unshaped* front neckline, repeat steps 3-5 for the front of the garment. Work to the same pattern row as the back and place the stitches on a holder.

Option 2. For a *shaped* front neckline, pick up stitches along the edge of one saddle only. Working back and forth, cast on stitches at the neck edge to shape the neck opening. How often and how many stitches you cast on here determines if the neck opening will be round or V-shaped. Having the neck opening charted out (see Figure 68), with lines drawn in to show where the cast-on stitches are added, often helps. End having worked a wrong-side row and place the stitches on a holder.

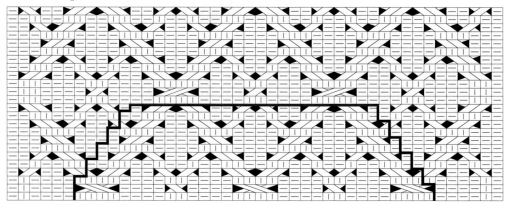

Fig. 68: *Chart showing neck shaping worked from the top down.*

Pick up stitches along the edge of the other saddle, and work the corresponding shaping on that side. End having worked a wrong-side row and place those stitches on a holder.

Reattach yarn to right front. Work across those stitches, cast on for the center front, then work across left front. Work front to match back, and end having worked a wrong-side row.

Step 7. Continue as appropriate for your chosen sleeve style.

For a dropped-shoulder Aran, go to to section 9.1.3.
For a peasant-sleeve Aran, go to to section 10.1.3.
For a set-in sleeve Aran, go to to section 11.1.2.

8.2.2.2 Top-Down Arans Without Saddles

In *Knitting From the Top*, Barbara Walker advises that top-down sweaters without saddles should begin with an invisible cast-on at the shoulder. The reasoning behind this advice is this: after knitting the back of the sweater, the knitter can pick up the stitches for the front of the sweater in the loops of the invisible cast-on, thus creating a seamless join at the shoulder.

I part company with Barbara Walker on this one. Not only is an invisible cast-on difficult to do neatly, Aran sweaters of any kind benefit from the additional stability provided by some sort of seam at the shoulder. All the weight of that heavily textured fabric hangs from the shoulder area. An invisible seam there simply doesn't provide enough structure to keep the garment from sagging out of shape. Forgo the invisible cast-on altogether and simply cast on and knit the back of the sweater. The stitches for the front will be picked up in the cast-on edge and provide plenty of stability.

Because there are no saddles to provide "drop" to the front neck opening, these styles must have shaped neckline openings.

Step 1. Cast on enough stitches to equal the body width measurement (if making a dropped-shoulder sweater) or the cross-shoulder measurement (if making a peasant- or set-in sleeve version).

Step 2 (Dropped-shoulder and peasant-sleeve versions). Establish the body pattern and work to the desired armhole depth. End having worked a wrong-side row and place those stitches on a holder.

Step 2 (Set-in sleeve version). Establish the body pattern and continue on all stitches to a point a few inches short of the desired armhole depth. Here, begin making increases (one stitch at each end of every other row) to add approximately half of the extra fabric needed to widen the cross-shoulder measurement to the body width measurement. When to begin adding these extra stitches depends on the difference between the cross-shoulder measurement and the body width measurement. If the difference between these two measurements is small (2-4"), begin increasing just a few inches short of the base of the armhole. If the difference is larger (5-8"), begin increasing farther from the base of the armhole. The remaining width needed will be cast on altogether at the base of the armhole opening.

Step 3. The left and right fronts are worked separately and joined after the neck shaping is complete. Pick up stitches for the right side of the neck opening (your right as you are wearing the sweater) in the cast-on edge of the back. Establish the pattern and shape the right front by casting on one or two stitches at the neck edge every other row. When the neck shaping on that side is complete, end having worked a wrong-side row and place the stitches on a holder.

Step 4. Repeat for the left side of the neck opening. Work to the same pattern row as the right front. End having worked a wrong-side row and place the stitches on a holder.

Step 5. Reattach yarn to the right front and knit across those stitches. Cast on stitches for the base of the neck opening, then knit across the stitches of the left front. Work the front to match the back, and end having worked a wrong-side row.

For a dropped-shoulder Aran, go to to section 9.2.3.
For a peasant-sleeve Aran, go to to section 10.2.3.
For a set-in sleeve Aran, go to section 11.2.2.

Dropped-Shoulder Arans

9

If you want to knit a seamless Aran with little or no shaping to track, this style is an excellent choice, whether knit bottom-up or top-down. Following is a list of design considerations you'll want to keep in mind as you work through the construction of this style of sweater:

• Composed mostly of rectangular shapes, dropped-shoulder Arans require minimal shaping. With careful placement of filler stitches and of the central cable pattern, shaping at the neck will not interfere with the cable patterns.

• One disadvantage of dropped-shoulder sweaters is that they aren't the most flattering sweater style for a lot of people. Aran sweaters, because of their heavy texture, are also prone to the problem of excess bulk under the arms. Modifying this style by making peasant sleeves (see Chapter 10) can help by moving the bulk of the body/sleeve seam closer to the body.

9.1 Dropped-Shoulder Arans With Saddles

This section covers three methods of knitting dropped-shoulder Arans with saddles. Begin by reading Chapter 8 — Constructing an Aran — for details on beginning each of these styles.

9.1.1 Knitting Bottom-up Flat Pieces

Begin by following Steps 1-3 in section 8.1.1. After completing step 3, continue as directed below:

Step 1. Place a marker at each edge to denote the beginning of the armhole openings. Work the back to the desired armhole depth, less half the saddle width. Make any decreases necessary to compensate for cable splay on the last row of the pattern.

> *Decision point*: Either bind off all stitches, or place them on a holder. Binding them off will require that the saddle be sewn to the body. Placing them on a holder lets you join the front and back to the saddles using a perpendicular join.

Step 2. Work the front of the piece to match the back, making the desired neck shaping, and finish as for the back.

Step 3. *Decision point:* Either knit the saddle and join it to the body simultaneously (Option 1 or 2), or knit the sleeve separately and sew it and the saddle into the body of the sweater (Option 3).

> Option 1. If the body stitches were left live, the saddle can simultaneously be knitted and joined to the body. Begin at the neck edge and work out to the shoulder. When all saddle and body stitches have been joined (end having knit a wrong-side saddle row), place the saddle stitches on a holder. Break the yarn, and reattach it at the marker on the edge of the body. Pick up stitches along the edge of the body, knit the saddle stitches from their holder, and pick up stitches along the other side of the body. Knit the sleeve down to the cuff.

> Option 2. Alternatively, knit the sleeve from the cuff to the shoulder. At the top of the sleeve, bind off all but the center saddle stitches. Continue knitting the saddle to the neck, simultaneously joining it to the body stitches.

Option 3. If the body stitches were bound off, knit the sleeve from the cuff to the shoulder. At the top of the sleeve, bind off all but the saddle stitches. Continue knitting the saddle to the neck. When the saddle is complete, sew it to the body.

Step 4. Repeat for second sleeve.

Step 5. Sew all seams and finish the neck opening.

9.1.2 Knitting Bottom-Up in the Round

Begin by following Steps 1-3 in section 8.1.2. After completing step 3, continue as directed below:

Step 1. Divide the work and place the stitches of the front on a holder. Working only on the stitches of the back, knit flat to the desired armhole depth, less half the saddle width. Make any decreases necessary to compensate for cable splay on the last row of the pattern.

> *Decision point*: Either bind off all stitches, or place them on a holder. Binding them off will require that the saddle be sewn to the body. Placing them on a holder lets you join the front and back to the saddles using a perpendicular join.

Step 2. Work the front of the piece to match the back, making the desired neck shaping, and finish as for the back.

Step 3. *Decision point:* Either knit the saddle and join it to the body simultaneously (Options 1 or 2), or knit the sleeve separately and sew it and the saddle into the body of the sweater (Option 3):

Option 1. If the body stitches were left live, the saddle can simultaneously be knitted and joined to the body. Begin at the neck edge and work out to the shoulder. When all saddle and body stitches have been joined (end having knit a wrong-side saddle row), place the saddle stitches on a holder. Break the yarn, and reattach it at the base of the armhole opening. Pick up stitches along the edge of the body, knit the saddle stitches from their holder, and pick up stitches along the other side of the body. Knit the sleeve down to the cuff.

Option 2. Alternatively, knit the sleeve from the cuff to the shoulder. At the top of the sleeve, bind off all but the center saddle stitches. Continue knitting the saddle to the neck, simultaneously joining it to the body stitches.

Option 3. If the body stitches were bound off, knit the sleeve from the cuff to the shoulder. At the top of the sleeve, bind off all but the saddle stitches. Continue knitting the saddle to the neck. When the saddle is complete, sew it to the body.

Step 4. Sew any seams and finish the neck opening.

9.1.3 Knitting From the Top

For a neckband-first version, begin by following Steps 1-9 in section 8.2.1. For a saddles-first version, begin by following Steps 1-7 in section 8.2.2.1. When those steps have been completed, continue as directed below:

Step 1. Knit across all stitches of the front.

Decision point: Continue across all stitches of the back, joining the front to the back. Knit the body in the round to the bottom of the sweater. Alternatively, mark the bases of the of the armholes on both the front and the back, then knit them separately to the bottom of the sweater. The body pieces will be seamed together later.

Step 2. Beginning at the left front armhole opening or marker, pick up and knit stitches for the sleeve along the left front edge of the body, then knit the saddle stitches from their holder, and pick up the remaining sleeve stitches along the left back body edge.

Decision point: Join the sleeve stitches and work in the round to the cuff. Alternatively, knit the sleeve flat and seam it later. Repeat for right sleeve.

Step 3. Sew any seams and, if necessary, finish the neck opening.

Schematic for dropped-shoulder Aran (with saddles)

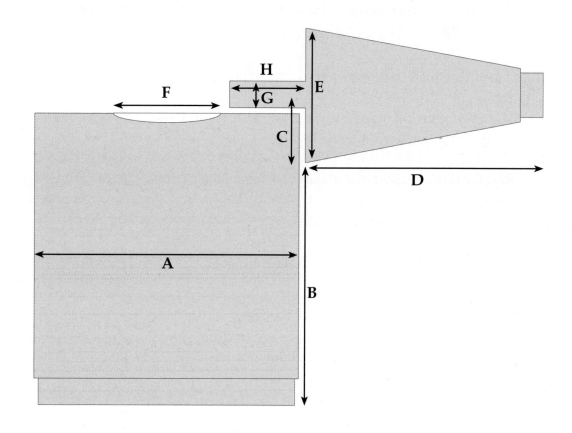

A   Width of sweater (½ the chest circumference plus desired ease)
B   Body length to armhole (this will depend on personal preference and row repeats
          of the chosen cable patterns)
C   Armhole depth
D   Sleeve length to underarm
E   Width at top of sleeve (equal to twice the armhole depth C)
F   Neckline opening
G   Width of saddle
H   Length of saddle

9.2 Dropped-Shoulder Arans Without Saddles

This section covers three methods of knitting dropped-shoulder Arans without saddles. Begin by reading Chapter 8—Constructing an Aran—for details on beginning each of these styles.

9.2.1 Knitting Bottom-up Flat Pieces

Begin by following Steps 1-3 in section 8.1.1. When those steps have been completed, continue as directed below:

Step 1. Place a marker at each edge to denote the beginning of the armhole openings. Work the back to the desired armhole depth. Make any decreases necessary to compensate for cable splay on the last row of the pattern.

> *Decision point*: Either bind off all stitches, or place them on a holder. Binding them off requires that the pieces be sewn together. Placing them on a holder lets you join the front and back using a three-needle bind-off.

Step 2. Work the front of the piece to match the back, making the desired neck shaping, and finish as for the back. Join the front and back.

Step 3. *Decision point:* Choose from one of these options for knitting the sleeves.

> Option 1. Pick up stitches between the markers along the edge of the body. Knit the sleeve down to the cuff.

> Option 2. Knit the sleeve from the cuff to the shoulder. At the top of the sleeve, bind off all stitches.

Step 4. Sew all seams and finish the neck opening.

9.2.2 Knitting Bottom-up in the Round

Begin by following Steps 1-3 in section 8.1.2. When those steps have been completed, continue as directed below:

Step 1. Divide the work and place the stitches of the front on a holder. Working only on the stitches of the back, knit to the desired armhole depth. Make any decreases necessary to compensate for cable splay on the last row of the pattern.

Decision point: Either bind off all stitches, or place them on a holder. Binding them off requires that the pieces be sewn together. Placing them on a holder lets you join the front and back using a three-needle bind-off.

Step 2. Work the front of the piece to match the back, making the desired neck shaping, and finish as for the back. Join the front and back.

Step 3. *Decision point:* Choose from one of these options for knitting the sleeves:

Option 1. Pick up stitches along the edge of the body around the armhole opening. Knit the sleeve down to the cuff.

Option 2. Knit the sleeve from the cuff to the shoulder. At the top of the sleeve, bind off all stitches.

Step 4. Sew any seams and finish the neck opening.

9.2.3 Knitting From the Top

Begin by following Steps 1-5 in section 8.2.2.2. When those steps have been completed, continue as directed below:

Step 1. Knit across all stitches of the front.

Decision point: Continue across all stitches of the back, joining the front to the back. Knit the body in the round to the bottom of the sweater. Alternatively, mark the bases of the of the armholes on both the front and the back, then knit them separately to the bottom of the sweater. The body pieces will be seamed together later.

Step 2. Beginning at the left front armhole opening or marker, pick up and knit stitches for the sleeve along the edge of the body.

Decision point: Join the sleeve stitches and work in the round to the cuff. Alternatively, knit the sleeve flat and seam it later. Repeat for right sleeve.

Step 3. Sew any seams and finish the neck opening.

Schematic for dropped-shoulder Aran (without saddles)

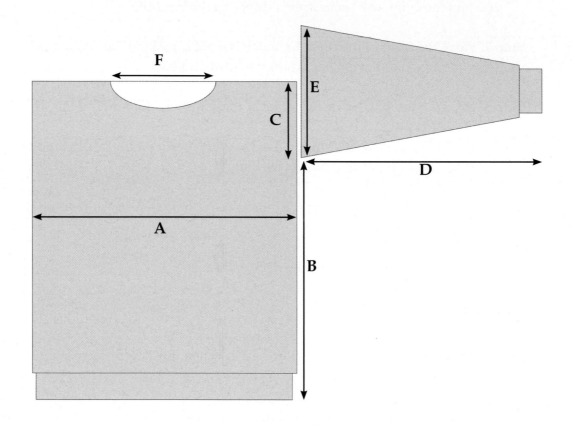

A   Width of sweater (½ the chest circumference plus desired ease)
B   Body length to armhole (this will depend on personal preference and row repeats
            of the chosen cable patterns)
C   Armhole depth
D   Length of sleeve
E   Width at top of sleeve (equal to twice the armhole depth C)
F   Neckline opening

10

Peasant Sleeve Arans

The peasant-sleeve style (also known as an indented sleeve or square set-in sleeve) has a fit closer to that of set-in sleeves, but does not require the same kind of math and mental gymnastics to design. When designing this kind of Aran sweater, keep the following points in mind:

• Although the body shape is primarily a rectangle, this style does have some shaping in the form of bound-off stitches at the base of the armhole. Plan for enough filler stitches at each side of the body in which that shaping can take place.

• This design is dependent upon accurate width at chest and cross-shoulder measurements. Ideally (except for larger-than-average sizes), the cross-shoulder measurement of the garment should be similar to the actual cross-shoulder body measurement of the wearer. This allows the sleeve/body seam to fall close to or along the shoulder line and makes for a better fit.

• The difference between the cross-shoulder measurement and the width at chest should be no more than approximately 6". For example, if the cross-shoulder measurement is 16" (for a ladies' medium sweater), the finished garment width at the chest can be up to 22" wide.

For garments where the width at chest needs to be more than 6" wider than the cross-shoulder measurement, increase the cross-shoulder measurement. For example, if the actual cross-shoulder measurement is 16" but the chest width is 26", increase the cross-shoulder measurement to 20".

This adjustment results in a garment which has more the appearance of a dropped-shoulder garment than of a set-in sleeve garment because the body of the garment does drop off the shoulder. The reasoning, however, is solid and has to do with the location of the sleeve-body seam when the garment is on the body. If the difference between the width at chest and the cross-shoulder measurement is greater than 6", the sleeve/body seam falls at an undesirable place on the female wearer's body.

• Note that peasant sleeves are longer than dropped-shoulder sleeves. This extra length matches the square indentation in the body.

10.1 Peasant-Sleeve Arans With Saddles

This section covers three methods of knitting peasant-sleeve Arans with saddles. Begin by reading Chapter 8—Constructing an Aran—for details on beginning each of these styles.

10.1.1 Knitting Bottom-up Flat Pieces

Begin by following Steps 1-3 in section 8.1.1. When those steps have been completed, continue as directed below:

Step 1. Bind off enough stitches at the beginning of the next two rows to decrease the body width measurement to the cross-shoulder measurement. For example, if the body width measurement is 20" and the cross-shoulder measurement is 16", then 4" worth of fabric needs to be removed—2" at each edge of the back piece.

Step 2. Work the back piece to the desired armhole depth less half the saddle width. Make any decreases necessary to compensate for cable splay on the last row of the pattern.

> *Decision point:* Either bind off all stitches, or place them on a holder. Binding them off will require that the saddle be sewn to the body. Placing them on a holder lets you join the front and back to the saddles using a perpendicular join.

Step 3. Work the front of the piece to match the back, making the desired neck shaping, and finish as for the back.

Step 4. *Decision point:* Either knit the saddle and join it to the body simultaneously (Option 1 or 2), or knit the sleeve separately and sew it and the saddle into the body of the sweater (Option 3).

> Option 1. If the body stitches were left live, the saddle can simultaneously be knitted and joined to the body. Begin at the neck edge and work out to the shoulder. When all saddle and body stitches have been joined (end having knit a wrong-side saddle row), place the saddle stitches on a holder. Break the yarn, and reattach it at the base of the square armhole. Pick up stitches along the vertical edge of the body, knit the saddle stitches from their holder, and pick up stitches along the other side of the body. Knit the sleeve down to the cuff.

Option 2. Alternatively, knit the sleeve from the cuff to the shoulder. At the top of the sleeve, bind off all but the center saddle stitches. Continue knitting the saddle to the neck, simultaneously joining it to the body stitches.

Option 3. If the body stitches were bound off, knit the sleeve from the cuff to the shoulder. At the top of the sleeve, bind off all but the saddle stitches. Continue knitting the saddle to the neck. When the saddle is complete, sew it to the body.

Step 5. Sew all seams and finish the neck opening.

10.1.2 Knitting Bottom–up in the Round

Begin by following Steps 1-3 in section 8.1.2. When those steps have been completed, continue as directed below:

Step 1. Divide the work and place the stitches of the front on a holder. Working only on the stitches of the back, bind off enough stitches at the beginning of the next two rows to decrease the body width measurement to the cross-shoulder measurement. For example, if the body width measurement is 20" and the cross-shoulder measurement is 16", then 4" worth of fabric needs to be removed—2" at each edge of the back piece.

Step 2. Work to the desired armhole depth, less half the saddle width. Make any decreases necessary to compensate for cable splay on the last row of the piece.

Decision point: Either bind off all stitches, or place them on a holder. Binding them off will require that the saddle be sewn to the body. Placing them on a holder lets you join the front and back to the saddles using a perpendicular join.

Step 3. Work the front of the piece to match the back, making the desired neck shaping, and finish as for the back.

Step 4. *Decision point:* Either knit the saddle and join it to the body simultaneously (Option 1 or 2), or knit the sleeve separately and sew it and the saddle into the body of the sweater (Option 3).

Option 1. If the body stitches were left live, the saddle can be simultaneously knitted and joined to the body. Begin at the neck edge and work out to the shoulder. When all saddle and body stitches have been joined (end having knit a wrong-side saddle row), place the saddle stitches on a holder. Break the yarn, and reattach it at the base of the square armhole. Pick up stitches along the edge of the body, knit the saddle stitches from their holder, and pick up stitches along the other side of the body. Knit the sleeve down to the cuff.

Option 2. Alternatively, knit the sleeve from the cuff to the shoulder. At the top of the sleeve, bind off all but the center saddle stitches. Continue knitting the saddle to the neck, simultaneously joining it to the body stitches.

Option 3. If the body stitches were bound off, knit the sleeve from the cuff to the shoulder. At the top of the sleeve, bind off all but the saddle stitches. Continue knitting the saddle to the neck. When the saddle is complete, sew it to the body.

Step 5. Sew any seams and finish the neck opening.

10.1.3 Knitting From the Top

For a neckband-first version, begin by following Steps 1-9 in section 8.2.1. For a saddles-first version, begin by following Steps 1-7 in section 8.2.2.1. When those steps have been completed, continue as directed below:

Step 1. *Decision point:* Either continue with the body (Option 1 or 2) or stop and work the sleeve (Option 3). Options 1 and 2 require that the underarm seam be sewn closed. Option 3 allows for a completely seamless garment, as the body stitches are picked up in the base of the sleeves.

Option 1. Working only on the stitches of the back, cast on enough stitches at the beginning of the next two rows to increase the cross-shoulder measurement to the body width measurement. For example, if the cross-shoulder measurement is 16" and the body width measurement is 20", an additional 2" of width needs to be added at each edge of the body (for a total of 4"). Continue knitting the back to the bottom of the sweater. Repeat for the front, then sew the front and back together at the sides.

Option 2. Knit across all stitches of the front. Cast on enough stitches here to increase the cross-shoulder measurement to the body width measurement. For example, if the cross-shoulder measurement is 16" and the body width measurement is 20", an additional 4" of width needs to be added at this underarm.

Work across the stitches of the back. Cast on enough stitches here to increase the cross-shoulder measurement to the body width measurement, as above. A total of 8" has been added to the circumference of the body—2" at each edge of the front and 2" at each edge of the back. Continue knitting to the bottom of the sweater.

Option 3. Leave the stitches for the front and back of the sweater on their holders. Beginning at the left front armhole opening, pick up and knit stitches for the sleeve along the left front edge of the body, knit the saddle stitches from their holder, then pick up and knit stitches for the sleeve along the left back edge. Knit the sleeve flat until it measures half the length needed to increase the cross-shoulder measurement to the body width measurement. For example, if the cross-shoulder measurement is 16" and the body width measurement is 20", knit the sleeve flat for 2".

At this point, either continue knitting the sleeve flat to the cuff, or join and knit it in the round. Repeat for the second sleeve.

When the sleeves are finished, return to the body. Knit across the stitches of the front, pick up stitches in the base of the sleeve, knit across the stitches of the back, then pick up stitches in the base of the other sleeve (see Figure 69). Continue knitting in the round on all stitches to the bottom of the sweater.

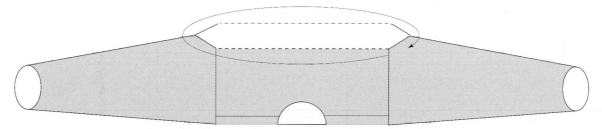

Fig. 69: *Picking up stitches to complete the body.*

Step 2. If you chose option 1 or 2, above, knit the sleeves once the body is complete. Beginning at the left front armhole opening or marker, pick up and knit stitches for the sleeve along the edge of the body, then knit the saddle stitches from their holder, and pick up the remaining sleeve stitches along the other body edge. Work until the sleeve measures the same as the width of the armhole indentation into the body, then begin the sleeve shaping and work down to the cuff.

Decision point: Join the sleeve stitches and work in the round to the cuff. Alternatively, knit the sleeve flat and seam it later. Repeat for right sleeve.

Step 3. Sew any seams and, if necessary, finish the neck opening.

Schematic for peasant-sleeve Aran (with saddles)

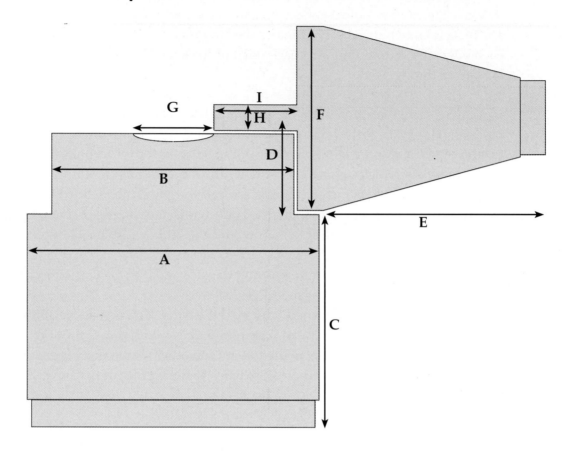

A   Width of sweater (½ the chest circumference plus desired ease)
B   Cross-shoulder measurement (does not usually include any ease except for larger-
        than-average sizes)
C   Body length to armhole (this will depend on personal preference and row repeats
        of the chosen cable patterns)
D   Armhole depth
E   Length of sleeve to underarm
F   Width at top of sleeve (equal to twice the armhole depth (D)
G   Neckline opening
H   Width of saddle
I   Length of saddle

10.2 Peasant-Sleeve Arans Without Saddles

This section covers three methods of knitting peasant-sleeve Arans without saddles. Begin by reading Chapter 8 — Constructing an Aran — for details on beginning each of these styles.

10.2.1 Knitting Bottom-up Flat Pieces

Begin by following Steps 1-3 in section 8.1.1. When those steps have been completed, continue as directed below:

Step 1. Bind off enough stitches at the beginning of the next two rows to decrease the body width measurement to the cross-shoulder measurement. For example, if the body width measurement is 20" and the cross-shoulder measurement is 16", then 4" worth of fabric needs to be removed — 2" at each edge of the back piece.

Step 2. Work the back to the desired armhole depth. Make any decreases necessary to compensate for cable splay on the last row of the pattern.

> *Decision point*: Either bind off all stitches, or place them on a holder. Binding them off requires that the pieces be sewn together. Placing them on a holder lets you join the front and back using a three-needle bind-off.

Step 3. Work the front of the piece to match the back, making the desired neck shaping, and finish as for the back.

Step 4. *Decision point:* Either pick up and knit the sleeve from around the edge of the armhole (Option 1) or knit the sleeve flat (Option 2).

> Option 1. Join the front and back at the shoulders. Beginning at the edge of one of the armhole openings, pick up and knit stitches for the sleeve along the edge of the body. Work until the sleeve measures the same as the width of the armhole indentation into the body, then begin the sleeve shaping and work down to the cuff.

> Option 2. Knit the sleeve flat, beginning with the cuff, and shaping the top of the sleeve to match the armhole indentation of the body. Sew the sleeve into the armhole opening.

Step 5. Sew any seams and finish the neck opening.

10.2.2 Knitting Bottom-up in the Round

Begin by following Steps 1-3 in section 8.1.2, Bottom-up Construction Knit in the Round. When those steps have been completed, continue as directed below:

Step 1. Divide the work and place the stitches of the front on a holder. Working only on the stitches of the back, bind off enough stitches at the beginning of the next two rows to decrease the body width measurement to the cross-shoulder measurement. For example, if the body width measurement is 20" and the cross-shoulder measurement is 16", then 4" worth of fabric needs to be removed—2" at each edge of the back piece.

Step 2. Work the back to the desired armhole depth. Make any decreases necessary to compensate for cable splay on the last row of the pattern.

> *Decision point*: Either bind off all stitches, or place them on a holder. Binding them off requires that the pieces be sewn together. Placing them on a holder lets you join the front and back using a three-needle bind-off.

Step 3. Work the front of the piece to match the back, making the desired neck shaping, and finish as for the back.

Step 4. Join the front and back at the shoulders. Beginning at the edge of one of the armhole openings, pick up and knit stitches for the sleeve along the edge of the body. Work back and forth until the sleeve measures the same as the width of the armhole indentation into the body. At that point, join and work the sleeve in the round to the cuff.

Step 5. Sew underarm seams and finish the neck opening.

10.2.3 Knitting From the Top

Begin by by following Steps 1-5 in section 8.2.2.2. When those steps have been completed, continue as directed below:

Step 1. *Decision point:* Either continue with the body (Option 1 or 2) or stop and work the sleeve (Option 3). Options 1 and 2 require that the underarm seam be sewn closed. Option 3 allows for a completely seamless garment, as the body stitches are picked up in the base of the sleeves.

Option 1. Working only on the stitches of the back, cast on enough stitches at the beginning of the next two rows to increase the cross-shoulder measurement to the body width measurement. For example, if the cross-shoulder measurement is 16" and the body width measurement is 20", an additional 2" of width needs to be added at each edge of the body (for a total of 4"). Continue knitting the back to the bottom of the sweater. Repeat for the front, then sew the front and back together at the sides.

Option 2. Knit across all stitches of the front. Cast on enough stitches here to increase the cross-shoulder measurement to the body width measurement. For example, if the cross-shoulder measurement is 16" and the body width measurement is 20", an additional 4" of width needs to be added at this underarm.

Work across the stitches of the back. Cast on enough stitches here to increase the cross-shoulder measurement to the body width measurement, as above. A total of 8" has been added to the circumference of the body—2" at each edge of the front and 2" at each edge of the back. Continue knitting to the bottom of the sweater.

Option 3. Leave the stitches for the front and back of the sweater on their holders. Beginning at the left front armhole opening, pick up and knit stitches for the sleeve along the edge of the body. Knit the sleeve flat until it equals half the amount needed to increase the cross-shoulder measurement to the body width measurement. For example, if the if the cross-shoulder measurement is 16" and the body width measurement is 20", knit the sleeve flat for 2".

At this point, either continue knitting the sleeve flat to the cuff, or join and knit it in the round. Repeat for the second sleeve.

When the sleeves are finished, return to the body. Knit across the stitches of the front, pick up stitches in the base of the sleeve (see Figure 69), knit across the stitches of the back, then pick up stitches in the base of the other sleeve. Continue knitting in the round on all stitches to the bottom of the sweater.

Step 2. If you chose option 1 or 2, above, knit the sleeves once the body is complete. Beginning at the left front armhole opening, pick up and knit stitches for the sleeve along the edge of the body. Work until the sleeve measures the same as the width of the armhole indentation into the body, then begin the sleeve shaping and work down to the cuff.

Decision point: Join the sleeve stitches and work in the round to the cuff. Alternatively, knit the sleeve flat and seam it later. Repeat for right sleeve.

Step 3. Sew any seams and finish the neck opening.

Schematic for peasant-sleeve Aran (without saddles)

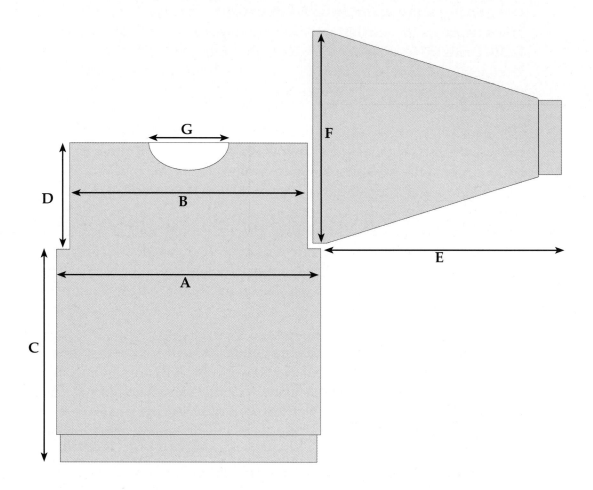

A   Width of sweater (½ the chest circumference plus desired ease)
B   Cross-shoulder measurement (does not usually include any ease except for larger-
          than-average sizes)
C   Body length to armhole (this will depend on personal preference and row repeats
          of the chosen cable patterns)
D   Armhole depth
E   Length of sleeve to underarm
F   Width at top of sleeve (equal to twice the armhole depth D)
G   Neckline opening

Set-In Sleeve Arans

11

Back when I was in college (in the mid '80s) and getting a lot of my fundamental experience in knitting and designing, the trend was toward boxy, dropped-shoulder garments. The thinking was that they were easier to knit and design because they didn't have fussy set-in sleeves and other tailoring details. Fortunately, no one ever told me that set-in sleeves were difficult, so many of the first dozen sweaters I ever knit were set-in sleeve designs.

Keep in mind the following design considerations when planning a set-in sleeve Aran sweater:

• Decide whether you want your sweater to have a standard set-in sleeve or a shallow set-in sleeve. A standard set-in sleeve—because it more closely adheres to the actual shape of the body—has a dressier appearance. A shallow set-in sleeve, which is usually combined with a slightly oversized body silhouette, has a more casual appearance. The shallow set-in sleeve works well when saddles are also part of the design.

• Sweaters with set-in sleeves have shaped armholes. Plan to have enough filler stitches at the armhole edges of the front and back pieces to accommodate the shaping required in this area. It's much easier to shape a garment in a filler stitch than in a cable pattern.

• The cross-shoulder measurement of this design (B on schematic) is very important. The difference between the width at chest (A) and the cross-shoulder measurement (B) will determine how to shape the base of the armhole and the armhole opening. If the difference between the chest width and the cross-shoulder measurement is significant (*e.g.*, 4-6"), plan to bind off more stitches at the underarm area and carry the decreases farther into the armhole shaping than if the difference between those two measurements were smaller. It's always good practice to take a sweater which fits the intended wearer well and take target measurements from that garment. This works best if the existing sweater is knit in the same (or similar) weight yarn as the sweater being designed.

• For larger-than-average sizes (*e.g.*, those needing to fit wearers with bust measurements larger than 44" around), the following adjustments may need to be made:

1. First, increase the cross-shoulder measurement. For example, if the cross-shoulder measurement is 16" but the chest width is 26", increase the cross-shoulder

measurement to 20" or even more (this is where referencing an existing sweater will come in handy). The body of the garment will drop off the shoulder a bit, but combined with the shaped sleeve cap, this approach provides a much better fit with less underarm bulk than a dropped-shoulder or even peasant-sleeve style.

2. Second, deepen the armhole opening to 10-13" (again, reference an existing sweater to determine the desired armhole depth). Armhole openings for smaller sizes may only be 7-9" deep, which doesn't allow enough room to keep the sleeve from binding on larger sizes.

3. Lastly, plan for a sleeve cap which is shallower and broader than a standard sleeve cap. The cross-shoulder measurement of this style is slightly wider than the actual cross-shoulder measurement of the intended wearer, and the armhole depth just a bit deeper. The sleeve cap is designed to be correspondingly shallower (only 2-4" tall) and broader.

• Garments with set-in sleeves generally have sloped shoulders, to follow the natural line of the human body. The shoulder section is divided roughly into thirds, and shaped so that the section closest to the neck opening will have more rows in it than the middle section, which has more rows in it than the section closest to the sleeve. The slopes are shaped using stepped bind-offs or short rows. If using stepped bind-offs, slip the first stitch in each set of stitches to be bound off, which will help to minimize the stair-step effect. If shaping with short rows, try to place each wrap-and-turn so that it falls within the background stitches between cables where it will be less noticeable.

• Filler stitches on either side of a central panel on the sleeves will allow for cap shaping without disturbing the cable pattern. It is possible to have cabling over the entire sleeve, although the cap shaping will be a bit trickier to figure out due to the differing gauges of the cable patterns.

11.1 Set-In Sleeve Arans With Saddles

It's rare to see saddles (which tend to be a casual style) paired with set-in sleeves (which tend to me more refined). However, do not let that stop you from combining the two. I've found that combining saddles with shallow set-in sleeve in a slightly oversized silhouette works well.

This section covers two methods of knitting set-in sleeve Arans with saddles. Begin by reading Chapter 8 — Constructing an Aran — for details on beginning each of these styles.

11.1.1 Knitting Bottom-up Flat Pieces

Begin by following Steps 1-3 in section 8.1.1.When those steps have been completed, continue as directed below:

Step 1. At the beginning of the next two rows, bind off one-quarter of the stitches required to decrease the body width measurement to the cross-shoulder measurement. For example, if the body width measurement is 20" and the cross-shoulder measurement is 16", bind off 1" worth of fabric at the beginning of each of the next two rows.

Continue to shape the armhole by decreasing one stitch at each edge until the width of the piece matches the cross-shoulder measurement.

Step 2. Work the back piece to the desired armhole depth less half the width of the saddles. Shape the shoulders with short rows or stepped bind-offs, making any decreases necessary to compensate for cable splay on the last row of the pattern.

Decision point: Either bind off all stitches, or place them on a holder. Binding them off will require that the saddle be sewn to the body. Placing them on a holder lets you join the front and back to the saddles using a perpendicular join.

Step 3. Work the front of the piece to match the back, making the desired neck shaping, and finish as for the back.

Step 4. Knit the first sleeve from the cuff to the underarm. Shape the cap as descibed in Chapter 7. At the top of the cap, bind off all but the saddle stitches. If the body stitches were left live, continue knitting the saddle to the neck, simultaneously joining it to the body stitches; otherwise, knit the saddle, then sew it to the body. Repeat for the second sleeve.

Step 5. Sew all seams and finish the neck opening.

11.1.2 Knitting From the Top

For a neckband-first version, begin by following Steps 1-9 in section 8.2.1. For a saddles-first version, begin by following Steps 1-7 in section 8.2.2.1. When those steps have been completed, continue as directed below:

Step 1. *Decision point:* It's entirely possible to knit set-in sleeves from the top down. Barbara Walker has three variations of this style in her book *Knitting From the Top*. I've tried all of them out on sample Arans and will give you my observations on each method.

The only caveat I would offer is that the first of these methods requires familiarity with short rows. Before you cavalierly set off to knit a top-down Aran with set-in sleeves, I would remind you that short rows in stockinette stitch are quite different from short rows in a pattern stitch. This is not meant to dissuade you, only to caution you to watch carefully as you knit (and if you plan to publish the design later, to take excellent notes).

Option 1, Circularly-Knit Set-in Sleeve. When the armhole shaping is complete, cast on any additional stitches needed for the base of the armhole and join the front and back. Continue on all stitches of the body to the bottom.

Return to an armhole. Beginning at the underarm seam, pick up the necessary number of stitches around the armhole opening. Place markers to divide the stitches around the opening into thirds.

Now, rather than working in the round, turn and work back to a point ⅔ of the way around the sleeve (there should be a marker here). Stop, make a short row wrap if desired, then turn and work back to the other marker. Make another short-row wrap, then work back to one stitch beyond the point where you stopped the first time, picking up and working the previous wrap if desired. Continue in this manner, working back and forth and always working one stitch more than you worked on the previous row, until you have incorporated all the stitches picked up around the opening except for the stitches in the flat section at the base of the armhole. On the last row, work across those stitches and all the way around the sleeve. Continue knitting the sleeve in the round to the cuff. Repeat for second sleeve.

Option 2, Flat Set-in Sleeve. This method seems to work best when it is combined with a shallow set-in sleeve. My version is somewhat different from Barbara Walker's because it does not use short rows.

When the armhole shaping is complete, pick up stitches along the unshaped portion of the side edge of the body and from the saddle stitches on holders (Figure 70). Work back and forth, picking up an additional stitch in the edge of the body on every row until there are no more body stitches in which to pick up sleeve stitches. Cast on stitches for the base of the armhole. Continue knitting the sleeve flat, or join and work in the round. When the sleeves are complete, reattach the yarn and knit the body (either working back and forth or in the round) to the bottom.

The advantage to picking up the stitches rather than working the shaping with short rows is obvious: the picked-up stitches are worked easily into the existing patterning.

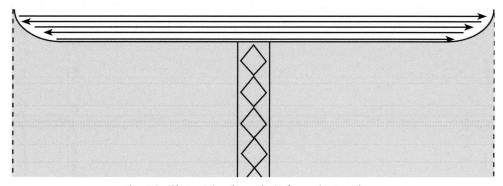

Fig. 70: *Flat set-in sleeve knit from the top down.*

Option 3, Simultaneous Set-in Sleeve. This variation is for knitters who like to amaze and dazzle their knitting friends (non-knitting friends just won't care). It's my favorite of all three of these methods. I did it once just to see if it could be done and the result was entirely amazing. Unfortunately, it's complicated enough that I haven't ever designed and written a pattern for it. (Advice to budding designers: designing a sweater is often the easiest part of the process. Writing the pattern so that someone else can recreate it is much tougher.)

Knit the body as described in Section 8.2 until both front and back together measure about ⅓ of the distance around the armhole opening. For example, if the armhole opening measures 18" around, ⅓ of that distance would be 6". Make sure that both front and back end on the same wrong-side pattern row.

Work across all stitches of the front, place a marker, then pick up stitches for the sleeve along the edge of the body (Figure 71). It's a 90° turn here so it will be fiddly for a bit. Place a marker and work across all stitches of the back. Place a marker, then pick up stitches along the other side edge. Place a marker of a different color to denote the beginning of the round here.

Work in the round from this point, making increases on either side of the markers *within the sleeve sections only* (Figure 72). Make these four increases

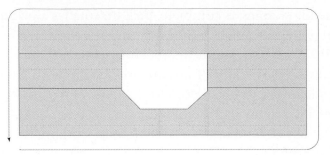

The measurement along this edge should equal about one-third of the distance around the armhole opening

Fig. 71: *Picking up stitches around the upper body for a simultaneous set-in sleeve.*

every other round to within a few inches of the desired armhole depth.

At that point, make increases on both side of the markers (in both body and sleeve sections) to shape the underarm curve.

Initially, make increases on the sleeve side of the markers only.

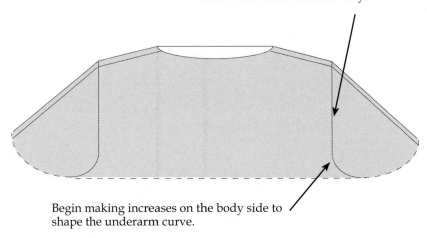

Begin making increases on the body side to shape the underarm curve.

Fig. 72: *Working the simultaneous set-in sleeve down to the base of the armhole.*

Divide the work into front, back, and sleeve sections. Knit across the stitches of front, cast on stitches for the base of the armhole, knit across the stitches of the back, then cast on stitches for the base of the other armhole. Continue working the body in the round to the bottom.

When the body is complete, finish knitting the sleeves, picking up stitches in the stitches which were cast on at the base of the armhole opening.

Step 2. Finish the neck opening, if necessary.

Schematic for shallow set-in sleeve Aran (with saddles)

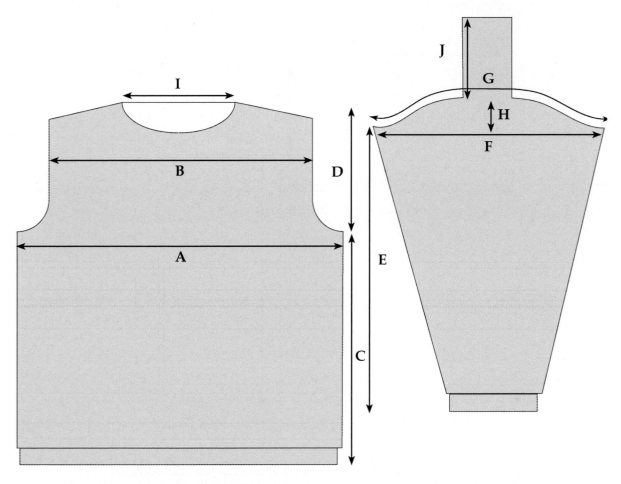

A   Width of sweater (one-half the chest circumference plus desired ease)
B   Cross-shoulder measurement
C   Body length to armhole (this will depend on personal preference and row repeats
        of the chosen cable patterns)
D   Armhole depth
E   Sleeve length to underarm
F   Width at top of sleeve (roughly equal to twice the armhole depth D)
G   Cap measurement (includes slight ease)
H   Height of cap
I   Neckline opening
J   Length of saddle

Schematic for standard set-in sleeve Aran (with saddles)

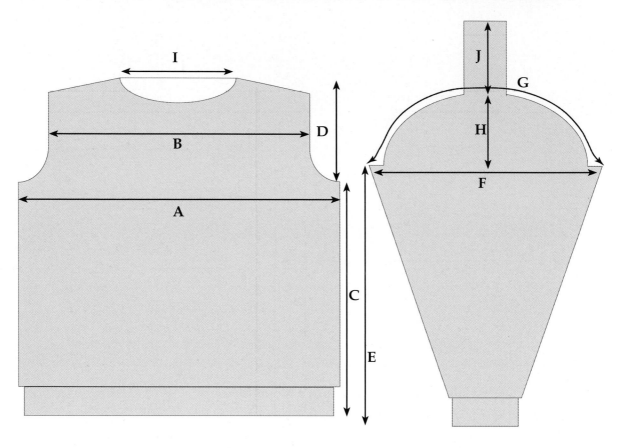

A   Width of sweater (one-half the chest circumference plus desired ease)
B   Cross-shoulder measurement (does not usually include any ease except for larger-
        than-average sizes)
C   Body length to armhole (this will depend on personal preference and row repeats
        of the chosen cable patterns)
D   Armhole depth
E   Sleeve length to underarm
F   Width at top of sleeve (roughly equal to twice the armhole depth D)
G   Cap measurement (includes slight ease)
H   Height of cap (should be approximately ⅔ of D)
I   Neckline opening
J   Length of saddle

11.2 Set-In Sleeve Arans Without Saddles

This section covers two methods of knitting set-in sleeve Arans with saddles. Begin by reading Chapter 8—Constructing an Aran—for details on beginning each of these styles.

11.2.1 Knitting Bottom-up Flat Pieces

Begin by following Steps 1-3 in section 8.1.1. When those steps have been completed, continue as directed below:

Step 1. At the beginning of the next two rows, bind off one-quarter of the stitches required to decrease the body width measurement to the cross-shoulder measurement. For example, if the body width measurement is 20" and the cross-shoulder measurement is 16", then bind off 1" worth of fabric at the beginning of each of the next two rows.

Continue to shape the armhole by decreasing one stitch at each edge until the width of the piece matches the cross-shoulder measurement.

Step 2. Work the back piece to the desired armhole depth. Shape the shoulders with short rows or stepped bind-offs, making any decreases necessary to compensate for cable splay on the last row of the pattern.

> *Decision point:* Either bind off all stitches, or place them on a holder. Binding them off requires that the pieces be sewn together. Placing them on a holder lets you join the front and back using a three-needle bind-off.

Step 3. Work the front of the piece to match the back, making the desired neck shaping, and finish as for the back.

Step 4. Knit the sleeves. Read the section on cap shaping for standard and shallow set-in sleeves in Chapter 7.

Step 5. Sew all seams and finish the neck opening.

11.2.2 Knitting From the Top

Begin by following Steps 1-5 in Section 8.2.2.2. When those steps have been completed, continue as directed below:

Step 1. *Decision point:* Follow the instructions for knitting one of the variations of sleeves from the top down in Section 11.1.2.

Step 2. When the sleeves are complete, finish knitting the body (if it hasn't already been completed).

Step 3. Finish the neck opening.

Schematic for shallow set-in sleeve Aran (without saddles)

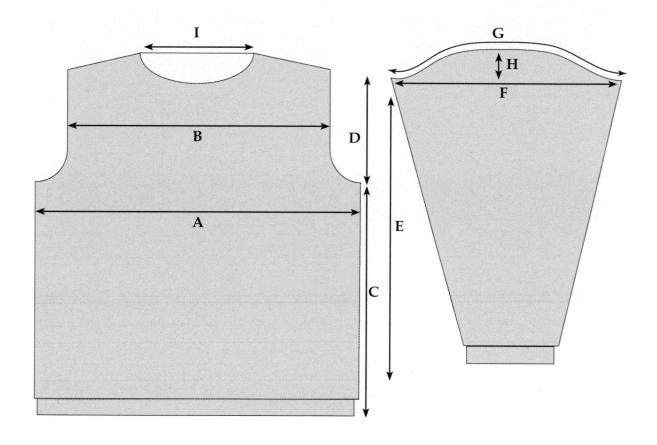

A   Width of sweater (one-half the chest circumference plus desired ease)
B   Cross-shoulder measurement
C   Body length to armhole (this will depend on personal preference and row repeats
            of the chosen cable patterns)
D   Armhole depth
E   Sleeve length to underarm
F   Width at top of sleeve (roughly equal to twice the armhole depth D)
G   Cap measurement (includes slight ease)
H   Height of cap
I   Neckline opening

Schematic for standard set-in sleeve Aran (without saddles)

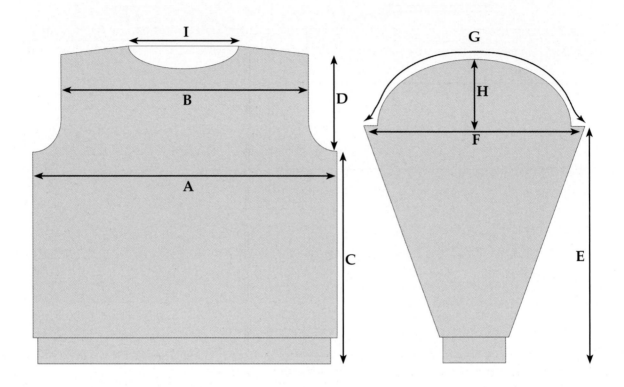

A   Width of sweater (one-half the chest circumference plus desired ease)
B   Cross-shoulder measurement (does not usually include any ease except for larger-than-average sizes)
C   Body length to armhole (this will depend on personal preference and row repeats of the chosen cable patterns)
D   Armhole depth
E   Sleeve length to underarm
F   Width at top of sleeve (roughly equal to twice the armhole depth D)
G   Cap measurement (includes slight ease)
H   Height of cap (should be approximately ⅔ of D)
I   Neckline opening

12

Raglan Sleeve Arans

Most of the commercially designed and knitted Arans I've seen have been raglan styles. Making the raglan decreases fit neatly into the cable patterning can be tricky, but because raglans are a flattering garment style for many people, they're worth the extra bit of effort. When designing a raglan Aran, keep the following points in mind:

• Should the sweater be knit in pieces or in the round? Knitting a raglan Aran in pieces requires that you keep careful track of the cable pattern and raglan shaping on each piece to ensure that they match up when sewn together. When knitting in the round, the cable crosses and decreases are worked on all pieces at the same time, automatically ensuring that the cables and shaping match perfectly.

• The raglan lines along which shaping takes place are made can be a design element in themselves. Usually the raglan shaping takes place along a column of plain knit stitches, but shaping can also take place in the purl ditches on either side of a narrow cable.

• It's especially important to "mirror" the cables on either side of the center pattern. The raglan shaping will be mirrored on either side of the garment, and it is easier to decrease into the cables if they cross in opposite directions.

12.1 Knitting Bottom-up in the Round

It's easiest to figure the calculations for this type of sweater knit in the round based on a percentage system (see *Knitting Without Tears* or *The Sweater Workshop* for good, solid examples of sweaters knitted using a percentage system). All shaping in the sweater is based on a percentage of a specific number: the circumference of the sweater, or the wearer's chest measurement plus the desired ease.

In a plain Stockinette Stitch sweater, the circumference number would be expressed in stitches. For example, a sweater 40 inches around knit at a gauge of 5 stitches per inch would have a circumference number of 200 stitches. All other stitch counts—the number of stitches to cast on for the ribbing, the number of stitches in the upper sleeve, *etc.*—are percentages of that circumference number.

However, an Aran sweater might be made up of four or five cable patterns and a filler stitch pattern, each with differing stitch gauges. Taking a percentage of the stitch count in the body (which likely has cable patterns with a condensed gauge) to figure the stitch count in the upper sleeve (which likely is knit in a filler stitch with a looser gauge) would probably result in an overly large sleeve. For Arans, it's more accurate to express the circumference number in inches. Use the percentage system to determine the size of each portion of the sweater in inches, then multiply by that portion's gauge to determine a stitch count.

As an example, suppose the body of a raglan sweater measures 40 inches. Taking 35% of this circumference number, we know the upper sleeve needs to be 14" around. Multiplying by the filler stitch gauge of 5 stitches per inch reveals that the upper sleeve should have 70 stitches.

12.2 Knitting From the Top

Top-down raglan sweater patterns are fairly easy to find. Many knitters like this method of construction because it's fun to knit and easy to check the fit as work progresses. Applied to Arans, though, this method is one of the trickier ones, and to be honest, if I wanted a raglan Aran sweater, I would knit it from the bottom up.

The reason? When knitting a raglan Aran from the bottom up, the decreases "eat into" already-established cable patterns. Little by little the cable patterns disappear into the raglan shaping.

In a top-down raglan Aran, on the other hand, stitches are added to the body of the sweater in the form of increases on either side of the raglan line. The knitter must not only keep track of the raglan shaping but also keep track of what happens to the additional stitches—are they worked as knits or purls on the next round? how does the cable pattern emerge from the raglan shaping? are there now enough stitches to work a cable crossing? and so on. Charting the yoke of the sweater can help, although it doesn't guarantee that there won't be some ripping and re-knitting necessary. Barbara Walker's book *Knitting From the Top* provides guidance for knitting top-down raglan sweaters, should you choose to try this method.

In short, knitting this style of Aran sweater requires a lot of advance planning and quiet time for concentrated knitting. Try it if you're looking for a challenge, but if all you want is a raglan Aran sweater, knit it from the bottom up.

Schematic for raglan Aran knit in the round

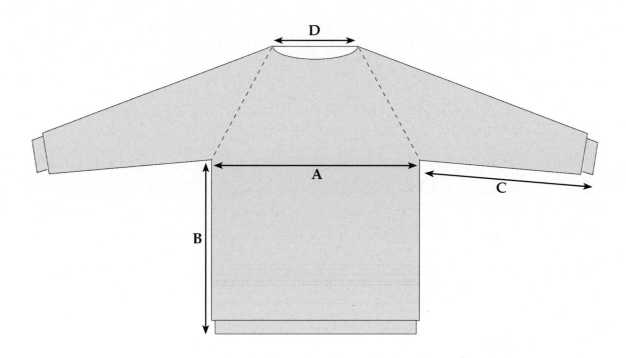

A   Width of sweater (½ the chest circumference plus desired ease)
B   Body length to armhole (this will depend on personal preference and row repeats
           of the chosen cable patterns)
C   Sleeve length to underarm
D   Neckline opening (5-9" depending upon style and size)

Both crew-neck and V-neck vests are interesting projects and often easier than attempting a full-blown Aran as a first design. A V-neck cardigan vest can be an elegant addition to anyone's wardrobe. Following is a list of design considerations to keep in mind when planning an Aran vest:

• Vests usually have shaped armholes. Plan to have enough filler stitches at the armhole edges of the front and back pieces to accommodate the decreasing required to shape them. It's much easier to shape a garment in a filler stitch than in a cable pattern.

• The cross-shoulder measurement (B on schematic) is very important in this style. The finished cross-shoulder measurement of the vest should be slightly narrower than the actual body measuremen, because the depth of the armhole trim will contribute to the finished cross-shoulder measurement of the vest. For example, if the finished cross-shoulder width of the vest will be 16" (which includes 1" of ribbing at each armhole opening), the cross-shoulder measurement of the vest before the armhole ribbing is added needs to be 14". Vests tend to look sloppy if the upper body and armhole ribbing fall off the shoulders.

   If all the filler stitches at the sides of the body are removed during the armhole shaping, the cable pattern running vertically along the armhole opening makes a nice detail.

• Vests generally have sloped shoulders, to follow the natural line of the human body. The shoulder section is divided roughly into thirds, and shaped so that the section closest to the neck opening will have more rows in it than the middle section, which has more rows in it than the section closest to the sleeve.

   The slopes are shaped using stepped bind-offs or short rows. If shaping with stepped bind-offs, slip the first stitch in each set of stitches to be bound off, which will help to minimize the stair-step effect. If shaping with short rows, try to place each wrap-and-turn so that it falls within the background stitches between cables.

• A V-neckline requires careful consideration of the center panel of the design. Options are to choose a cable which will end gracefully at the point where the V-neck shaping begins; to choose one which will "split" and travel up either side of the neck opening; or to use a filler stitch (such as Trinity Stitch) as the center panel.

   Keep a close eye on the shaping as it "eats into" existing cables. Remember that it is possible to cross a cable even if it doesn't contain the required number of stitches. For example, if the cable has three stitches are crossing over three stitches but shaping has left only five stitches over which to cross the cable, make it a three-stitch-over-two-stitch cross instead (see Chapter 7 for more information).

13.1 Aran Vests—With or Without Saddles

Aran vests are essentially set-in sleeve Arans without the sleeves. Follow any of the construction methods in Chapter 11, making the armhole slightly deeper to accomodate the armhole trim.

Saddles are occasionally found in vest designs. Because the cable used in the saddle is not carried down a sleeve, it's used more as an accent. For that reason, choose a cable of appropriate width and length for this area of the vest.

Schematic for crew- or V-neck Aran vest (without saddles)

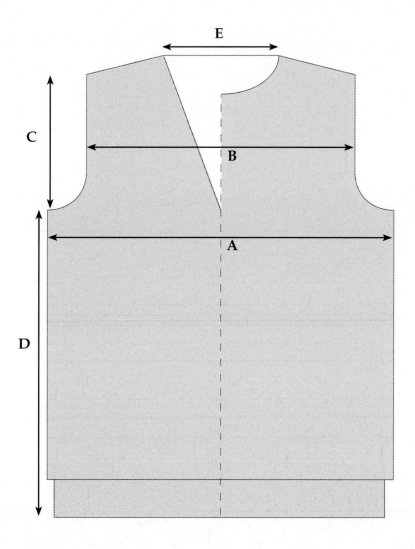

A   Width of vest (one-half the chest circumference plus desired ease)

B   Cross-shoulder measurement (does not usually include any ease)

C   Armhole depth

D   Body length to armhole (this will depend on personal preference and row repeats
          of the chosen cable patterns)

E   Neckline opening

Schematic for crew- or V-neck Aran vest (with saddles)

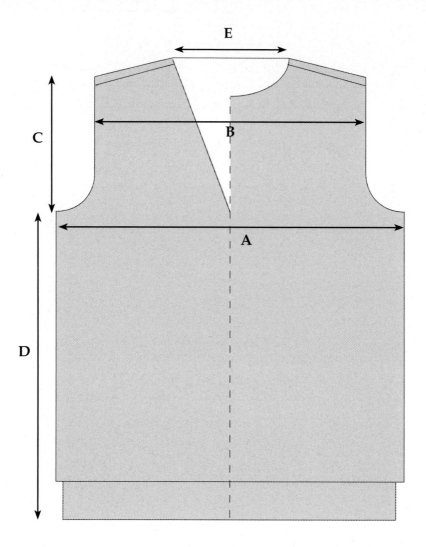

A   Width of vest (one-half the chest circumference plus desired ease)
B   Cross-shoulder measurement (does not usually include ease)
C   Armhole depth
D   Body length to armhole (this will depend on personal preference and row repeats
        of the chosen cable patterns)
E   Neckline opening

T-Sleeve Arans

14

This style is certainly a "non-traditional" Aran style. However, it is fun to design and knit and can be a great way to show off cabling skills. The saddle in this style is actually just a sleeve which extends across the entire top of the body from cuff to cuff.

Keep the following points in mind when planning a T-sleeve Aran sweater:

• The neck opening will fall right in the middle of the knitting. It may be necessary to chart out the cable patterning around the neck opening to ensure that the opening falls at an appropriate place in the row repeat.

• Because the saddle is knitted in one piece from cuff to cuff, choose cable patterns which are bidirectional.

• Wingspan measurement is crucial in this style. Wingspan is measured from cuff to cuff across the top of the back of the body, while the arms are slightly bent. Subtract the body width measurement from the wingspan measurement and divide the result in half to determine the length of each sleeve.

14.1 T-Sleeve Aran Construction

Step 1. Begin knitting at one cuff, adding stitches as the work progresses toward the shoulders. At the shoulders, the saddle should be twice as wide as the armhole openings are deep (D on schematic). For instance, if the armhole opening is 9" deep, the saddle needs to be 18" wide at the top, just before knitting the upper body portion. Mark the point at which the sleeve portion stops and the body portion of the saddle begins.

Step 2. Work the saddle until it measures the desired length from the shoulder to the begining of the neck opening. This length is determined by subtracting the width of the neck opening (E on schematic) from the body width measurement (A on schematic). Divide the remaining number in half to determine the length of the saddle from shoulder to neck opening.

Step 3. Start a neckline opening. This opening can be a simple rectangular shape, or can incorporate increases and decreases to create a more shaped opening.

If making a cardigan, bind off half the saddle stitches when the neck shaping is half complete, then cast them on again on the next row.

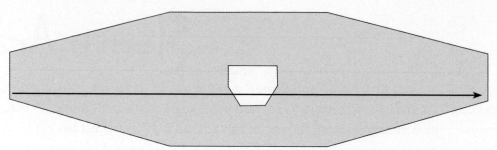

Fig. 73: *Working the top of the T-Sleeve Aran from one cuff to the other.*

Step 4. Continue knitting the second half of the saddle, shaping the other half of the neck opening to correspond to the first half. Place a marker to denote the end of the body portion, and continue to the cuff.

Step 5. Once the saddle is complete, sew the sleeve seams up to the markers. Pick up the body stitches in the edges of the saddle and knit the body in the round to the bottom.

Schematic for T-sleeve Aran

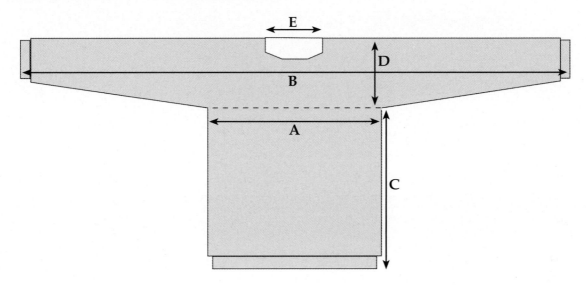

A   Width of sweater (½ the chest circumference plus desired ease)

B   Wingspan measurement (from cuff to cuff across the back, arms slightly bent)

C   Body length to armhole (this will depend on personal preference and row repeats
         of the chosen cable patterns)

D   Armhole depth

E   Neckline opening

Wide-Saddle Arans

15

Normally, saddles should not be wider than about 2-3", because the presence of the saddle drops the neckline on both the front and back of a sweater. Too wide a saddle will drop the back neckline unattractively.

This style, however, has saddles knit in such a way that the back neck drop is not an issue. Thus, the saddles can be the center of attention—use them as a wonderful place to show off your cabling skills. These designs are also quite striking when the saddles and body are done in contrasting colors. This style has two versions: in the first version, the saddle extends across the back neck opening; in the second version, the saddle extends across both the front and back neck openings.

Following is a list of design considerations to keep in mind when planning a wide-saddle Aran sweater:

- Choose a wide cable panel or a combination of narrower patterns for the saddle area of these styles. Aim for a saddle width of about 8".

- Because each half of the saddle begins at the center back of the sweater and is worked outward, the cable pattern chosen does not have to be bidirectional.

15.1 Wide-Saddle Version #1

Like the traditional top-down saddle shoulder sweater, this sweater begins by determining the length of the saddles. Subtract the neck opening from the total body width measurement (for a dropped-shoulder version) or the cross-shoulder measurement (for a peasant- or set-in sleeve sweater). Divide the result in half to determine the length of each saddle. For example, if the body width of a dropped-shoulder sweater is 22" and the neck opening is 8", the saddles each will be 7" long.

Step 1. Begin at the center back neck on half the number of stitches which will be required for the saddle. Knit the saddle to half the width of the neck opening (*e.g.*, if the neck opening will be 8" wide, knit the saddle to 4").

Step 2. Cast on the other half of the saddle stitches and knit until the saddle reaches the desired length (Figure 74). Place those stitches on a holder.

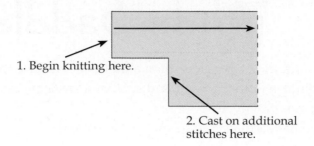

1. Begin knitting here.

2. Cast on additional
stitches here.

Fig. 74: *Beginning the wide-saddle Aran, version #1.*

Step 3. Pick up stitches in the initial cast-on edge of the first saddle, and knit the second saddle the same way (Figure 75). Place those stitches on a holder.

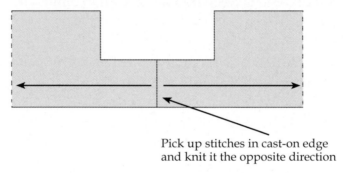

Pick up stitches in cast-on edge
and knit it the opposite direction

Fig. 75: *Knitting the second half of the
wide-saddle Aran, version #1.*

Step 4. From this point, continue as for a top-down Aran, incorporating either a dropped-shoulder, peasant-, or set-in sleeve. The neckline may be shaped further, but keep in mind that the width of the saddle already provides a significant amount of drop to the front neckline.

15.2 Wide-Saddle Version #2

Like the Wide-Saddle Version #1, the saddle knitting begins at the center neck and works outward toward the shoulders. However, unlike the first version which had only a back saddle piece, this version has both front and back saddle pieces which are knit separately and joined when the neck shaping is complete. This style will take a considerable bit of advance planning.

Step 1. Knit two saddle pieces for the front and back neck openings separately. Work them until each measures half the width of the neck opening (*e.g.*, if the neck opening is 8" wide, knit each piece to 4"). The pieces can be identical, or the back one can be wider than the front one. If the back piece is wider than the front piece, the neck opening will sit lower in front than in back.

Step 2. Knit across the first saddle piece, cast on stitches for the neck opening, then knit across the other saddle piece. Continue on this joined piece until the saddle measures the desired length (Figure 76).

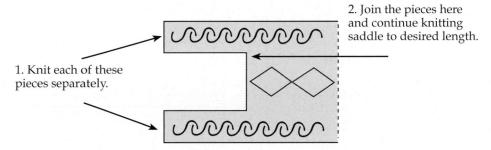

Fig. 76: *Beginning the wide-saddle Aran saddle, version #2.*

If desired, make the neck opening rounder by increasing stitches on the neck opening sides of the two individual saddle pieces before joining them.

Step 3. Continue as for Version #1, picking up stitches for the other saddle in the initial cast-on row of the first saddle. Work the second saddle to the desired length.

Step 4. From this point, continue as for a top-down Aran, incorporating either a dropped-shoulder, peasant-, or set-in sleeve.

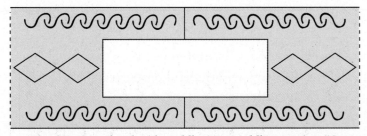

Fig. 77: *Completed wide-saddle Aran saddles, version #2.*

Schematic for wide-saddle Aran (version #1) with dropped-shoulder sleeves

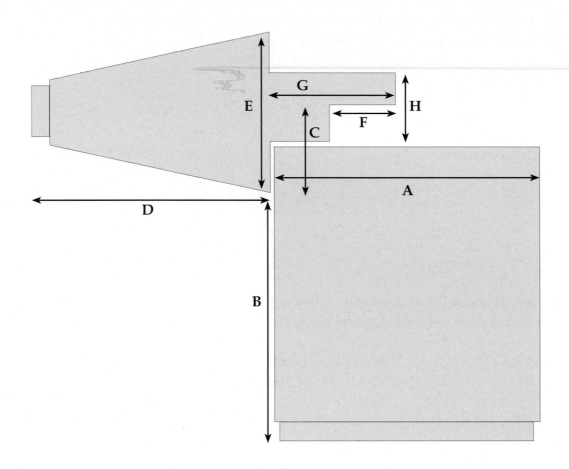

A   Width of sweater (½ the chest circumference plus desired ease)
B   Body length to armhole (this will depend on personal preference and row repeats of the chosen cable patterns)
C   Armhole depth
D   Sleeve length to underarm
E   Width at top of sleeve (equal to twice the armhole depth C)
F   One-half neckline opening
G   Length of saddle
H   Width of saddle

Schematic for wide-saddle Aran (version #2) with dropped-shoulder sleeves

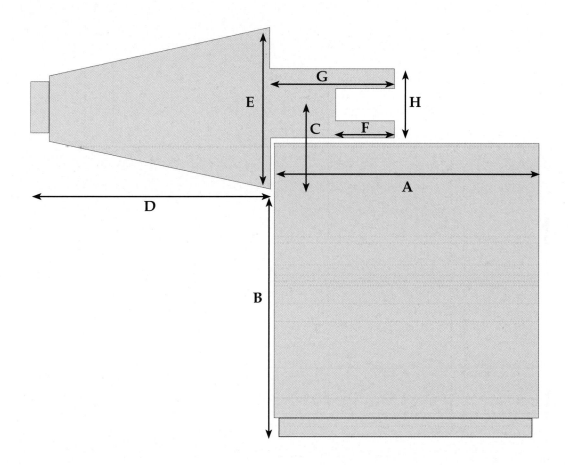

A   Width of sweater (½ the chest circumference plus desired ease)
B   Body length to armhole (this will depend on personal preference and row repeats
            of the chosen cable patterns)
C   Armhole depth
D   Sleeve length to underarm
E   Width at top of sleeve (equal to twice the armhole depth C)
F   One-half neckline opening
G   Length of saddle
H   Width of saddle

Part Three

Aran Sweater Projects

Aran Vest Project

Design Notes: This vest is intended to be a very feminine wardrobe addition. Vests are wonderfully versatile and can be worn alone or under a jacket, dressed up or dressed down.

The cables I chose for this design are in keeping with the feminine look—a braid panel in the center adds texture without overwhelming the design, and the small wishbone and delicate knot cable provide visual interest. The design is framed with a simple k1, p1 ribbing.

Level of Experience: Intermediate

Sizes: S, M, L

Finished Measurements:
Width at chest: 19 (21, 23)"
Length to underarm: 14"
Armhole depth: 9 (9½, 10)"

Materials:
1200 (1400, 1600) yards any yarn which knits to the
    specified gauge. Sample done in Jo Sharp DK
    wool (100% wool, 109 yds/50g skein)
US sizes #5 (3¾ mm) and #6 (4 mm) 16" and 24"
    circular needles or size required to obtain
    gauge
Cable needle
Stitch markers
Five ½" buttons

Gauge: 26 sts and 32 rows = 4" (10 cm) over Hurdle
Rib stitch on US size #6 (4 mm) needles

Hurdle Rib (over an odd number of sts):

Row 1 (WS): *P1, k1; rep from *, end p1
Rows 2 and 3: Knit
Row 4: *K1, p1; rep from *, end k1

DIRECTIONS

Back: Using smaller needles, cast on 141 (155, 169) sts. Work in k1, p1 ribbing (begin and end each RS row with a knit st) for 1", end having worked a WS row. On the next row, knit all sts, inc 15 (17, 19) sts evenly across row—156 (172, 188) sts.

Change to larger needles and est patt as foll (WS): 19 (27, 35) sts Hurdle Rib, k1, 8 sts chart/patt A, 4 sts chart/patt B, 14 sts chart/patt C, 4 sts chart/patt B, 8 sts chart/patt A, 40 sts chart/patt D, 8 sts chart/patt A, 4 sts chart/patt B, 14 sts chart/patt C, 4 sts chart/patt B, 8 sts chart/patt A, k1, 19 (27, 35) sts Hurdle Rib.

Cont in patt as est until Back measures 14" or desired length. End having worked a WS row.

Shape armholes: Bind off 10 (16, 20) sts at beg of next 2 rows, then dec one st at each armhole edge every other row 9 (11, 15) times—118 sts. Cont in patt as est until armhole measures 9 (9½, 10)" or desired depth.

Shape shoulders: Bind off 13 sts at beg of next four rows. Bind off remaining sts, working 10 decreases across chart/patt D as you bind off.

Left Front (your left as you are wearing the garment): Using smaller needles, cast on 63 69, 75) sts and work in k1, p1 ribbing for 1", end having worked a WS row. On the next row, knit all sts, inc 7 (11, 15) sts evenly across row—70 (80, 90) sts.

Change to larger needles and est patt as foll (WS): Work 11 (13, 15) sts Hurdle Rib, k1, 8 sts chart/patt A, 4 sts chart/patt B, 14 sts chart/patt C, 4 sts chart/patt B, 8 sts chart/patt A, k1, 19 (27, 35) sts Hurdle Rib. Cont in patt as est until Left Front measures same as Back to armhole. End having worked a WS row.

Shape armhole: Bind off 10 (16, 20) sts at beg of next row, then dec one st at armhole edge every other row 9 (11, 15) times, AND AT SAME TIME, dec one st at neck edge every 3 rows 18 (20, 22) times—33 sts. Work even until Left Front measures same as Back. Shape shoulders same as Back.

Right Front: Using smaller needles, cast on 63 (69, 75) sts and work in k1, p1 ribbing for 1", end having worked a WS row. On the next row, knit all sts, inc 7 (11, 15) sts evenly across row — 70 (80, 90) sts.

Change to larger needles and est patt as foll (WS): Work 19 (27, 35) sts Hurdle Rib, k1, 8 sts chart/patt A, 4 sts chart/patt B, 14 sts chart/patt C, 4 sts chart/patt B, 8 sts chart/patt A, k1, 11 (13, 15) sts Hurdle Rib. Cont in patt as est until Right Front measures same as Back to armhole. End having worked a RS row.

Shape armhole: Bind off 10 (16, 20) sts at beg of next row, then dec one st at armhole edge every other row 9 (11, 15) times, AND AT SAME TIME, dec one st at neck edge every 3 rows 18 (20, 22) times — 33 sts. Work even until Right Front measures same as Back. Shape shoulders same as Back.

Assembly: Sew shoulder and side seams. With smaller needles, pick up and knit 335 (339, 343) sts along Right Front edge, across Back neck, and down Left Front edge. Work in k1, p1 ribbing for ½". Mark placement of five ⅝" buttons along Left Front edge. On next row of ribbing, work five ½" buttonholes on Right Front edge to correspond to placement of buttons. Cont in k1, p1 ribbing for an additional ½". Bind off loosely in pattern.

With smaller needles, pick up and knit 108 (114, 120) sts around armhole opening. Work in k1, p1 ribbing for 1" or desired depth. Bind off loosely in pattern. Repeat for second armhole.

Finishing: Sew buttons opposite buttonholes. Darn in all ends. Wash and block according to yarn manufacturer's recommendations.

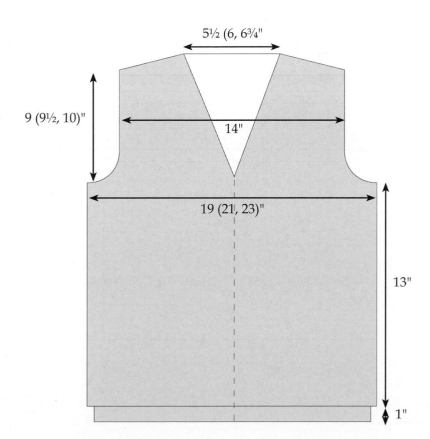

Chart A

3

1

4

2

Pattern for Chart A

Rows 1 and 3 (WS): K1, p6, k1
Row 2: P1, 1/2 LC, 1/2 RC, p1
Row 4: P1, k2, RT, k2, p1

Chart B

1

2

Pattern for Chart B

Row 1 (WS): K1, p2, k1
Row 2: P1, 1/1 RC, p1

Chart C

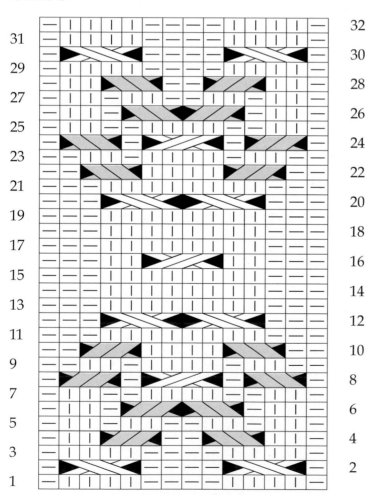

31
29
27
25
23
21
19
17
15
13
11
9
7
5
3
1

32
30
28
26
24
22
20
18
16
14
12
10
8
6
4
2

Pattern for Chart C

Rows 1, 3, 29, and 31 (WS): K1, p4, k4, p4, k1
Rows 2 and 30: P1, 2/2 LC, p4, 2/2 LC, p1
Row 4: P1, k2, 2/1 LPC, p2, 2/1 RPC, k2, p1
Rows 5 and 27: [K1, p2] twice, k2, [p2, k1] twice
Row 6: P1, k2, p1, 2/1 LPC, 2/1 RPC, p1, k2, p1
Rows 7 and 25: K1, p2, k2, p4, k2, p2, k1
Row 8: P1, 2/1 LPC, p1, 2/2 RC, p1, 2/1 RPC, p1
Rows 9 and 23: K2, p2, k1, p4, k1, p2, k2
Row 10: P2, 2/1 LPC, k4, 2/1 RPC, p2
Rows 11, 13, 15, 17, 19, and 21: K3, p8, k3
Rows 12 and 20: P3, [2/2 LC] twice, p3
Rows 14 and 18: P3, k8, p3
Row 16: P3, k2, 2/2 RC, k2, p3
Row 22: P2, 2/1 RPC, k4, 2/1 LPC, p2
Row 24: P1, 2/1 RPC, p1, 2/2 RC, p1, 2/1 LPC, p1
Row 26: P1, k2, p1, 2/1 RPC, 2/1 LPC, p1, k2, p1
Row 28: P1, k2, 2/1 RPC, p2, 2/1 LPC, k2, p1
Row 32: P1, k4, p4, k4, p1

Pattern for Chart D

Rows 1 and all WS rows: [k1, p2] thirteen times, k1
Rows 2 and 6: [P1, k2] thirteen times, p1
Row 4: [P1, 2/1/2 RPC] six times, p1, k2, p1
Row 8: P1, k2, p1, [2/1/2 LPC, p1] six times

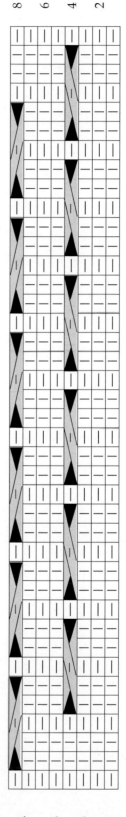

Chart D

Aran Pullover Project ¹⁷

Design Notes: I wanted this design to include those elements I think of when I visualize the quintessential Aran design—saddle shoulders, big bold cables, Aran-weight yarn. This design has those elements and more. The top-down peasant-sleeve construction make this a good first Aran sweater project. It may also inspire you to try designing your very first Aran.

Level of Experience: Ambitious Beginner to Intermediate

Sizes: Men's XS, S, M, L, XL

Finished Measurements:
Width at chest: 18 (20, 22, 24, 26)"
Length to underarm: 13 (14, 15½, 17, 18½)"
Armhole depth: 9 (9½, 10, 10½, 11)"
Sleeve length to underarm: 20 (20, 19, 18, 17)"

Materials:
1800 (2000, 2200, 2400, 2600) yards any yarn which knits to the specified gauge. Sample done in Jamieson's Aran (100% wool, 152 yds/100g skein)
US size #7 (4½ mm) and #6 (4 mm) 16" and 24" circular needles or size required to obtain gauge
Cable needles
Stitch holders

Gauge: 18 sts and 24 rows = 4" (10 cm) over Moss Stitch on US size #7 (4½ mm) needles

Moss Stitch (over an even number of sts):

Row 1 (WS): *P1, k1; rep from * to end
Rows 2 and 3: *K1, p1; rep from * to end
Row 4: *P1, k1; rep from * to end

DIRECTIONS

Saddles (make 2): Using larger needles, cast on 21 sts. Est patt as foll (WS): P1, 4 sts chart/patt D, 11 sts chart/patt B, 4 sts chart/patt D, p1. Cont in patt as est until saddle measures 5 (5, 5½, 6, 7)". End having worked a WS row, and place sts on holder.

Back: Pick up 36 (38, 38, 44, 48) sts along saddle edge, cast on 32 (32, 40, 40, 40) sts for back neck opening, pick up 36 (38, 38, 44, 48) sts along other saddle edge—104 (108, 116, 128, 136) sts. Est patt as foll (WS): Work 2 (4, 8, 14, 18) sts Moss Stitch, k1, 18 sts chart/patt A, 11 sts chart/patt B, 40 sts chart/patt C, 11 sts chart/patt B, 18 sts chart/patt A, k1, 2 (4, 8, 14, 18) sts Moss Stitch. Keeping first and last st of each RS row as knits and first and last st of each WS row as purls, cont in patt as est until Back measures 9 (9½, 10, 10½, 11)" when measured from center of saddle. End having worked a WS row, and place sts on holder.

Left Front (your left as you are wearing the sweater): Pick up 36 (38, 38, 44, 48) sts along edge of saddle. Est patt as foll (WS): Work 2 (4, 8, 14, 18) sts Moss Stitch, k1, 18 sts chart/patt A, 11 sts chart/patt B, 4 (4, 0, 0, 0) sts chart/patt C. Cont in patt as est, casting on an additional st at neck edge every other row 8 (8, 10, 10, 10) times, working cast-on sts into chart/patt C. End having worked a WS row, and place sts on holder.

Right Front: Work as for Left Front, reversing shaping. When Right Front measures same as Left Front (and they are on the same pattern row), work across sts of Right Front, cast on an additional 16 (16, 20, 20, 20) sts for base of neck opening, then knit Left Front sts from holder. Cont in patt as est until Front measures 9 (9½, 10, 10½, 11)" when measured from center of saddle (Back and Front should be on same pattern row). End having worked a WS row, and place sts on holder.

Sleeves (make 2): Pick up 36 (42, 42, 46, 46) sts along armhole edge, knit 21 sts of saddle from holder, pick up 36 (42, 42, 46, 46) sts along armhole edge—93 (105, 105, 113, 113) sts. Est patt as foll (WS): Work 36 (42, 42, 46, 46) sts Moss Stitch, 21 sts of saddle, 36 (42, 42, 46, 46) sts Moss Stitch. Keeping first and last sts of each RS row as knits and first and last sts of each WS row as purls, cont in patt as est until sleeve measures 1 (1½, 1½, 1½, 2)". End having worked a WS row.

One next row, join sts and cont knitting sleeve in the round. Keeping first and last sts of each rnd as knits, knit 4 rnds in patt as est. On next rnd, decrease 1 st on either side of those two knit sts. Cont to dec every 6th (4th, 4th, 4th, 4th) rnd 19 (21, 21, 21, 17) times more—53 (61, 61, 69, 77) sts. Work even until sleeve measures 18 (18, 17, 16, 15)" from underarm.

Change to smaller needles and knit one rnd, dec 11 (13, 13, 15, 17) sts evenly around—42 (48, 48, 54, 60) sts. Work in k1, p1 ribbing on these sts for 2" or desired depth. Bind off loosely in patt.

Body: Reattach yarn at center of right underarm. Pick up 6 (8, 8, 8, 10) sts in base of right sleeve, knit sts of Front from holder, pick up 12 (16, 16, 16, 20) sts in base of left sleeve, knit sts of Back from holder, pick up 6 (8, 8, 8, 10) sts in base of right sleeve—232 (248, 264, 288, 312) sts. Cont in patt as est, working picked-up sts in Moss Stitch, until Body measures 10½ (11½, 13, 14½, 16)" from underarm or desired length.

Change to smaller needles and knit one rnd, dec 46 (48, 52, 56, 62) sts around—186 (200, 212, 232, 250) sts. Work in k1, p1 ribbing on all sts for 2½". Bind off loosely in patt.

Neckband: With smaller ndls, pick up and knit 90 (90, 90, 96, 96) sts around neck opening. Work in k1, p1 ribbing for 1" or desired depth. Bind off loosely in patt.

Finishing: Darn in all ends. Wash and block according to yarn manufacturer's instructions.

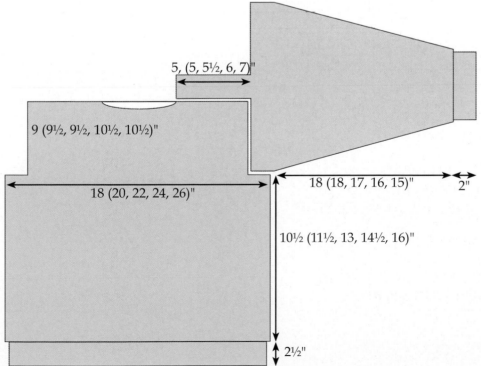

5, (5, 5½, 6, 7)"

9 (9½, 9½, 10½, 10½)"

18 (18, 17, 16, 15)"

2"

18 (20, 22, 24, 26)"

10½ (11½, 13, 14½, 16)"

2½"

Chart A

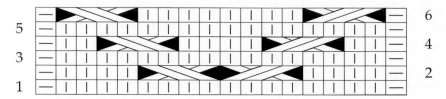

Pattern for Chart A

Rows 1, 3 and 5 (WS): K1, p16, k1
Row 2: P1, k4, 2/2 RC, 2/2 LC, k4, p1
Row 4: P1, k2, 2/2 RC, k4, 2/2 LC, k2, p1
Row 6: P1, 2/2 RC, k8, 2/2 LC, p1

Chart B

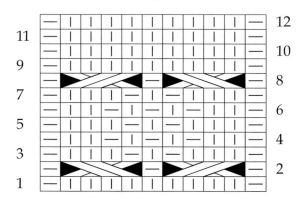

Pattern for Chart B

Rows 1, 9 and 11 (WS): K1, p9, k1
Row 2: P1, 2/2 RC, p1, 2/2 LC, p1
Rows 3, 5 and 7: K1, p3, k1, p1, k1, p3,
    k1
Rows 4 and 6: P1, k2, [p1, k1] twice, p1,
    k2, p1
Row 8: P1, 2/2 LC, p1, 2/2 RC, p1
Rows 10 and 12: P1, k9, p1

Pattern for Chart C

Row 1 and all WS rows: K1, [p2, k2] nine
    times, p2, k1
Rows 2, 6, 8, 10, 14 and 16: P1, [k2, p2] nine
    times, k2, p1
Row 4: P1, [2/2/2 RPC, p2] four times, 2/2/2
    RPC, p1
Row 12: P1, k2, [p2, 2/2/2 LPC] four times,
    p2, k2, p1

Chart D

1  2

Pattern for Chart D

Row 1 (WS): K1, p2, k1
Row 2: P1, 1/1 RC, p1

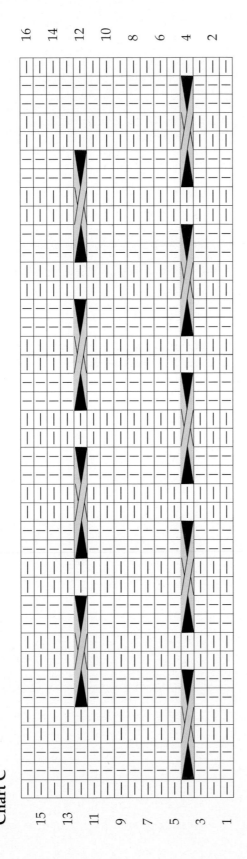

Chart C

Set-In Sleeve Aran Project

Design Notes: I wanted this to be a dressier-than-average Aran sweater. The cables are very delicate and I liked the way they interacted with each other. The set-in sleeves are definitely dressy. I took advantage of cable splay to make the bottom edge flare out a bit, giving the illusion of waist shaping.

Level of Experience: Intermediate

Sizes: XS, S, M, L, XL

Finished Measurements:
Width at chest: 18 (20, 22, 24, 26)"
Length to underarm: 17¾ (17¼, 19, 18½, 18)"
Armhole depth: 7 (7½, 8, 8½, 9)"
Sleeve length to underarm: 18 (17, 16, 15, 14)"

Materials:
1550 (1700, 2050, 2200, 2350) yards any yarn which knits to the specified gauge. Sample done in Jo Sharp DK wool (100% wool, 109 yds/50g skein)
US size #4 (3½ mm) and #5 (3¾ mm) 16" and 24" circular needles or size required to obtain gauge
Cable needle
Stitch holders

Gauge: 20 sts and 30 rows = 4" (10 cm) over Sand Stitch on US size #5 (3¾ mm) needles

Sand Stitch

Row 1 (WS): Knit
Row 2: *P1, k1; rep from * to end

DIRECTIONS

Back: Using smaller needles, cast on 130 (140, 150, 160, 170) sts. Work 6 rows Garter Stitch (knit every row), end having worked a RS row.

Change to larger needles and est patt as foll: 11 (16, 21, 26, 31) sts Sand Stitch, p1, 7 sts chart/patt A, 4 sts chart/patt B, 16 sts chart/patt C, 4 sts chart/patt B, 7 sts chart/patt A, 30 sts chart/patt D, 7 sts chart/patt A, 4 sts chart/patt B, 16 sts chart/patt C, 4 sts chart/patt B, 7 sts chart/patt A, p1, 11 (16, 21, 26, 31) sts Sand Stitch.

Cont in patt as est until piece measures 17¾ (17¼, 19, 18½, 18)" from cast-on edge.

Shape armholes: Bind off 4 (6, 8, 10, 12) sts at beg of next two rows, then one st at beg of next 8 (12, 16, 16, 16) rows—114 (116, 118, 124, 130) sts. Cont in patt as est until Back measures approx 7 (7½, 8, 8½, 9)" from beg of armhole shaping, ending with Row 9 of chart/patt D. Bind off 12 (12, 12, 12, 13) sts at beg of next four rows. Bind off rem 66 (68, 70, 76, 78) sts or place on holder.

Front: Work as for Back until Front measures approx 4 (4½, 5, 5½, 6)" from beg of armhole shaping, ending with Row 13 of chart/patt D. Work across 45 (46, 47, 49, 52) sts, bind off or place center 24 (24, 24, 26, 26) sts on holder for base of neck opening, then work across rem 45 (46, 47, 49, 52) sts. Working each side separately, bind off one st at neck edge every other row 5 (5, 5, 7, 7) times. Cont in patt as est until Front measures same as Back from beg of armhole shaping. Shape shoulders same as Back.

Sleeves (make 2): Using smaller needles, cast on 44 (44, 48, 48, 52) sts. Work 6 rows garter stitch (knit every row), end having worked a WS row. On next row, knit all sts, inc 8 (8, 10, 10, 10) sts evenly across row—52 (52, 58, 58, 62) sts.

Change to larger ndls and work all sts of sleeve in Sand Stitch for five rows. On next (RS) row, inc 1 st at each end, working increased sts into Sand Stitch pattern. Cont in patt as est, inc every 8th (6th, 6th, 4th, 4th) row 8 (10, 10, 12, 13) more times—70 (74, 80, 84, 90) sts. Work even until sleeve measures 18 (17, 16, 15, 14)" or desired length.

Shape cap: Bind off 4 (6, 8, 10, 12) sts at beg of next two rows, then one st at the beg of next 20 (22, 24, 12, 14) rows, then two sts at the beg of next 10 (12, 12, 12, 12) rows, then 5 (4, 4, 14, 14) sts at beg of next two rows, then 6 (4, 4, 0, 0) sts at beg of last two rows.

Finishing: Block pieces according to yarn manufacturer's instructions. Sew shoulder seams. Sew sleeves into armhole openings. Sew side seams. With smaller needles, pick up and knit 98 (104, 110, 116, 122) sts around neck opening. Work in garter stitch (knit one round, purl one round) for 1" or desired depth. Bind off loosely. Darn in all ends.

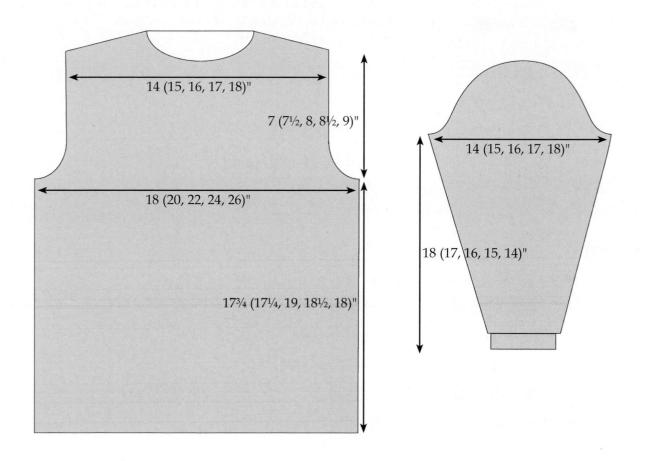

14 (15, 16, 17, 18)"

7 (7½, 8, 8½, 9)"

18 (20, 22, 24, 26)"

17¾ (17¼, 19, 18½, 18)"

14 (15, 16, 17, 18)"

18 (17, 16, 15, 14)"

Chart A

Pattern for Chart A

Rows 1, 3, and 5 (WS): K1, p5, k1
Rows 2 and 6: P1, k5, p1
Row 4: P1, 1/3/1 RC, p1

Chart B

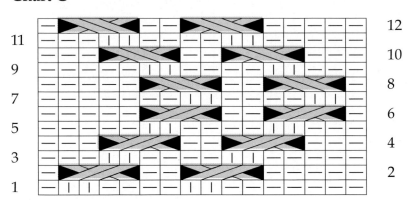

Pattern for Chart B

Row 1 (WS): K1, LPT, p1, k1
Row 2: P1, RT, k1, p1

Chart C

Pattern for Chart C

Row 1 (WS): K1, p2, k4, p2, k7
Row 2: P5, 2/2 RPC, p2, 2/2 RPC, p1
Row 3: K3, p2, k4, p2, k5
Row 4: P3, 2/2 RPC, p2, 2/2 RPC, p3
Row 5: K5, p2, k4, p2, k3
Row 6: P1, 2/2 RPC, p2, 2/2 RPC, p5
Row 7: K7, p2, k4, p2, k1
Row 8: P1, 2/2 LPC, p2, 2/2 LPC, p5
Row 9: K5, p2, k4, p2, k3
Row 10: P3, 2/2 LPC, p2, 2/2 LPC, p3
Row 11: K3, p2, k4, p2, k5
Row 12: P5, 2/2 LPC, p2, 2/2 LPC, p1

Chart D

Pattern for Chart D

Row 1 (WS): K1, p2, k2, p2, k4, p8, k4, p2, k2, p2, k1
Row 2: P1, k2, p2, k2, p4, k2, 2/2 RC, k2, p4, k2, p2, k2, p1
Row 3: K1, p2, k2, p2, k4, p8, k4, p2, k2, p2, k1
Row 4: P1, k2, p2, k2, p4, [2/2 LC] twice, p4, k2, p2, k2, p1
Row 5: K1, p2, k2, p2, k4, p8, k4, p2, k2, p2, k1
Row 6: [P1, 2/1 LPC] twice, p2, 2/1 RPC, 2/2 RC, 2/1 LPC, p2, [2/1 LPC, p1] twice
Row 7: [K2, p2] three times, k1, p4, k1, [p2, k2] three times
Row 8: P2, 2/1 LPC, p1, 2/1 LPC, [2/1 RPC] twice, [2/1 LPC] twice, 2/1 RPC, p1, 2/1 RPC, p2
Row 9: K3, p2, k2, p4, k1, p2, k2, p2, k1, p4, k2, p2, k3
Row 10: P3, 2/2 LPC, 2/2 RC, 2/1 RPC, p2, 2/1 LPC, 2/2 RC, 2/2 RPC, p3
Row 11: K5, p8, k4, p8, k5
Row 12: P5, [2/2 LC] twice, p4, [2/2 LC] twice, p5
Row 13: K5, p8, k4, p8, k5
Row 14: P5, k2, 2/2 RC, k2, p4, k2, 2/2 RC, k2, p5
Row 15: K5, p8, k4, p8, k5
Row 16: P5, [2/2 LC] twice, p4, [2/2 LC] twice, p5
Row 17: K5, p8, k4, p8, k5
Row 18: P3, 2/2 RPC, 2/2 RC, 2/1 LPC, p2, 2/1 RPC, 2/2 RC, 2/2 LPC, p3
Row 19: K3, p2, k2, p4, k1, p2, k2, p2, k1, p4, k2, p2, k3
Row 20: P2, 2/1 RPC, p1, 2/1 RPC, [2/1 LPC] twice, [2/1 RPC] twice, 2/1 LPC, p1, 2/1 LPC, p2
Row 21: [K2, p2] three times, k1, p4, k1, [p2, k2] three times
Row 22: [P1, 2/1 RPC] twice, p2, 2/1 LPC, 2/2 RC, 2/1 RPC, p2, [2/1 LPC, p1] twice
Row 23: K1, p2, k2, p2, k4, p8, k4, p2, k2, p2, k1
Row 24: P1, k2, p2, k2, p4, [2/2 LC] twice, p4, k2, p2, k2, p1

Design Notes: I find raglan Arans to be one of the most challenging styles to design. For this sweater, I chose an intricate lattice design for the center back. Knowing that it would be difficult to split that cable pattern, I substituted Moss Stitch in its place on the front of the cardgian. The other cables act as counterpoint to the sharp angles of the lattice pattern.

I chose to work a simple 4-stitch cable along the raglan lines. The sweater is knit from the bottom up, with the sleeves joined at the underarm.

Level of Experience: Intermediate to Advanced

Sizes: S, M, L, XL

Finished Measurements:
Width at chest: 18½ (20½, 22½, 24½)"
Length to underarm: 12 (13, 14, 15)"
Sleeve length to underarm: 18 (17, 16, 15)"

Materials:
1500 (1700, 2000, 2300) yards any yarn which
    knits to the specified gauge. Sample done in
    Jo Sharp DK wool (100% wool, 109 yds/50g
    skein)
US size #4 (3½ mm) 16" and 24" circular and
    dpns or size required to obtain gauge
Cable needle
Stitch markers
Stitch holders
Seven ⅝" buttons

Gauge: 25 sts and 34 rows = 4" (10 cm) over Moss Stitch on US size #4 (3½ mm) needles

Moss Stitch (over an even number of stitches):

Row 1 (WS): *K1, p1; rep from *
Rows 2 and 3: *P1, k1; rep from *
Row 4: *K1, p1; rep from *

Moss Stitch (over an odd number of stitches):

Row 1 (WS): *K1, p1; rep from *, end k1
Row 2: *k1, p1; rep from *, end k1
Rows 3 and 4: *P1, k1; rep from *, end p1

DIRECTIONS

Body: Cast on 259 (277, 295, 317) sts. Work in k1, p1 ribbing for 2½" or desired depth. On last RS row of ribbing, inc 29 (31, 33, 35) sts evenly — 288 (308, 328, 352) sts.

Est patt as foll (WS): Work 15 (17, 19, 19) sts Moss Stitch, k1, 11 sts chart/patt A, 22 sts chart/patt B, 11 sts chart/patt A, k1, 8 (12, 16, 22) sts Moss Stitch, place marker, 8 (12, 16, 22) sts Moss Stitch, k1, 11 sts chart/patt A, 22 sts chart/patt B, 11 sts chart/patt A, 44 sts chart/patt C, 11 sts chart/patt A, 22 sts chart/patt B, 11 sts chart/patt A, k1, 8 (12, 16, 22) sts Moss Stitch, place marker, 8 (12, 16, 22) sts Moss Stitch, k1, 11 sts chart/patt A, 22 sts chart/patt B, 11 sts chart/patt A, k1, 15 (17, 19, 19) sts Moss Stitch.

Cont in patt as est until body measures 12 (13, 14, 15)" or desired length to underarm. On last WS row, work across 58 (63, 68, 73) sts of Left Front, place next 22 (24, 26, 28) sts on holder for underarm, work across 128 (134, 140, 150) sts of Back, place next 22 (24, 26, 28) sts on holder for underarm, then work across rem 58 (63, 68, 73) sts of Right Front.

Sleeves (make 2): Cast on 72 (72, 82, 88) sts. Join, being careful not to twist, and work k1, p1 ribbing for 2½" or desired depth. On last rnd of ribbing, inc 18 (18, 20, 22) sts evenly around — 90 (90, 102, 110) sts.

Est patt as foll: Work 33 (33, 39, 43) sts Moss Stitch, p1, work 22 sts chart/patt B, p1, work 33 (33, 39, 43) sts Moss Stitch. Place marker to denote beg of rnds. Cont in patt as est, inc one st on either side of marker every 10 (7, 7, 6) rnds 12 (16, 14, 15) times — 114 (122, 130, 140) sts. Cont until sleeve measures 18 (17, 16, 15)" or desired length. After working last rnd, place 22 (24, 26, 28) sts (half from either side of marker) onto holder for underarm.

Join body and sleeves (RS): Cont in patt as est, work across 56 (61, 66, 71) sts of Right Front, place marker, k2, knit first 2 sts of Sleeve, place marker, work across 88 (94, 100, 108) sts of Sleeve, place marker, k2, knit first 2 sts of Back, place marker, work across 124 (130, 136, 146) sts of Back, place marker, k2, knit first 2 sts of other Sleeve, place marker, work across 88 (94, 100, 108) sts of Sleeve, place marker, k2, knit first 2 sts of Left Front, place marker, knit across rem 56 (61, 66, 71) sts of Left Front—428 (456, 484, 520) sts. The sts between the markers will be worked in chart/patt D (mirror chart/patt D on either side of the body to make working the decrease rows easier).

Cont in patt as est for 7 (7, 3, 3) more rows.

Next RS row: *Work to within one st of marker. Slip this st to RH needle, remove marker, then slip st back to LH needle. Work a k2tog here with this st and the first st of chart/patt D. Work the next 2 sts of chart/patt D. Slip the last st of chart/patt D to the RH needle, remove marker, then slip st back to LH needle. Work an SSK with the last st of chart/patt D and the next st on needle.

Repeat from *, working the decreases on either side of chart/patt D the same way on the remainder of the row. Replace the markers if desired, or mark all sts of chart/patt D with a large safety pin and move it up as work progresses.

Work one row even.

The next row should be a decrease row *and* a cable crossing row. Work to within one st of chart/patt D. Slip this st to RH needle. Work the cable crossing, incorporating the st to be decreased into the cable as follows:

> If working a 2/2 Left Cross, slip the next 2 sts to a cable needle and hold them at the front of the work. Work a k2tog with the next st on the LH needle and the st which was slipped to the RH needle, then k1. Knit the first st from the cable needle, then work an SSK with the second st on the cable needle and the next body st.

> If working a 2/2 Right Cross, slip the next 2 sts to a cable needle and hold them at the back of the work. Work a k2tog with the next st and the st which was slipped to the RH needle, then k1. Knit the first st from the cable needle, then work an SSK with the second st on the cable needle and the next body st.

Cont to dec in this manner every other row until a total of 32 (36, 40, 44) decrease rows have been worked.

Shape neck (RS): Bind off 9 (10, 11, 12) sts at beg of next two rows. Cont to work raglan decs as est, AND AT SAME TIME, bind off one st at neck edge every other row 7 times. End having worked a WS row. Break yarn.

Neckband: With RS facing and beg at Right Front neck edge, pick up 20 sts along Right Front neck edge, knit sts from working ndl, then pick up and knit 20 sts from Left Front edge. Work in k1, p1 ribbing on all sts for 1" or desired depth. Bind off loosely in patt.

Buttonband: Using smaller needles, pick up and knit 121 (127, 133, 139) sts along Left Front edge. Work in k1, p1 ribbing for 1". Bind off loosely in patt. Mark placement of seven ⅝" buttons along Left Front edge.

Buttonhole band: Pick up and knit 121 (127, 133, 139) sts along Right Front edge. Work in k1, p1 ribbing for ½". On next row of ribbing, work seven evenly-spaced buttonholes on Right Front edge to correspond to placement of buttons. Cont in k1, p1 ribbing for an additional ½". Bind off loosely in patt.

Finishing: Sew buttons opposite buttonholes. Graft underarm sts together. Darn in all ends. Wash and block according to yarn manufacturer's instructions.

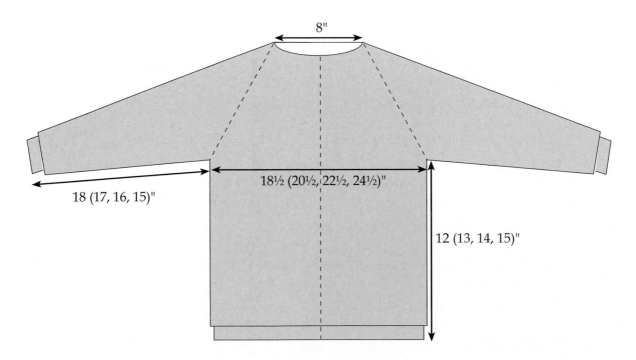

Chart A

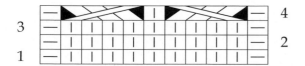

Pattern for Chart A

Row 1 (WS): K1, p9, k1
Row 2: P1, k9, p1
Row 3: K1, p9, k1
Row 4: P1, 1/3 LC, k1, 1/3 RC, p1

Chart B

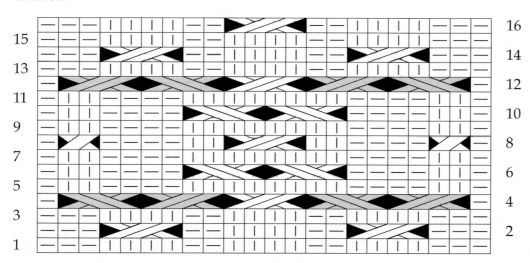

Pattern for Chart B

Rows 1, 3, 13, and 15 (WS): K3, p4, [k2, p4] twice, k3
Rows 2 and 14: P3, 2/2 RC, p2, k4, p2, 2/2 RC, p3
Row 4: P1, 2/2 RPC, 2/2 LPC, 2/2 RC, 2/2 RPC, 2/2 LPC, p1
Rows 5, 7, 9, and 11: K1, p2, k4, p8, k4, p2, k1
Rows 6 and 10: P1, k2, p4, [2/2 LC] twice, p4, k2, p1
Row 8: P1, 1/1 RC, p4, k2, 2/2 RC, k2, p4, 1/1 RC, p1
Row 12: P1, 2/2 LPC, 2/2 RPC, 2/2 RC, 2/2 LPC, 2/2 RPC, p1
Row 16: P3, k4, p2, 2/2 RC, p2, k4, p3

Pattern for Chart C

Row 1 (WS): K1, p1, [k4, p4, k4, p2] twice, k4, p4, k4, p1, k1
Row 2: P1, k1, [p4, 2/2 LC, p4, 1/1 LC] twice, p4, 2/2 LC, p4, k1, p1
Row 3 and all other WS rows: Knit the knits and purl the purls
Row 4: P1, 1/1 LPC, [p2, 2/1 RPC, 2/1 LPC, p2, 1/1 RPC, 1/1 LPC] twice, p2, 2/1 RPC,
    2/1 LPC, p2, 1/1 RPC, p1
Row 6: [P2, 1/1 LPC, 2/1 RPC, p2, 2/1 LPC, 1/1 RPC] three times, p2
Row 8: P3, [2/1 RC, p4, 2/1 LC, p4] twice, 2/1 RC, p4, 2/1 LC, p3
Row 10: [P2, 2/1 RPC, 1/1 LPC, p2, 1/1 RPC, 2/1 LPC] three times, p2
Row 12: P1, [2/1 RPC, p2, 1/1 LPC, 1/1 RPC, p2, 2/1 LPC] three times, p1
Row 14: P1, k2, [p4, 1/1 RC, p4, 2/2 RC] twice, p4, 1/1 RC, p4, k2, p1
Row 16: P1, [2/1 LPC, p2, 1/1 RPC, 1/1 LPC, p2, 2/1 RPC] three times, p1
Row 18: [P2, 2/1 LPC, 1/1 RPC, p2, 1/1 LPC, 2/1 RPC] three times, p2
Row 20: P3, [2/1 LC, p4, 2/1 RC, p4] twice, 2/1 LC, p4, 2/1 RC, p3
Row 22: [P2, 1/1 RPC, 2/1 LPC, p2, 2/1 RPC, 1/1 LPC] three times, p2
Row 24: P1, 1/1 RPC, [p2, 2/1 LPC, 2/1 RPC, p2, 1/1 LPC, 1/1 RPC] twice, p2, 2/1 LPC,
    2/1 RPC, p2, 1/1 LPC, p1

Chart D

Pattern for Chart D

Rows 1 and 3 (WS): Purl
Row 2: 2/2 RC
Row 4: Knit

Chart C

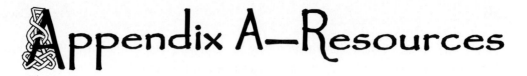

Appendix A—Resources

The following list of resources, categorized by subject, will be helpful as you design and plan your Aran sweaters.

Stitch Dictionaries

Big Book of Knitting Stitch Patterns, Sterling Publishing Company, 2000.

Harmony Guide to Knitting Stitches, Lyric Books, 1983.

Harmony Guide to 440 More Knitting Stitches, Lyric Books, 1990.

Harmony Guide to Practical Knitting Stitches, Lyric Books, 1990.

Harmony Guide to Aran Knitting, Lyric Books, 1991.

Klöpper, Gisela, *Beautiful Knitting Patterns*, Sterling Publishing Company, 2003.

Maloney, Annie, *The Cable Knitting Handbook*, self-published, 2004.

Stanfield, Lesley, *The New Knitting Stitch Library*, Chilton, 1992.

Walker, Barbara, *A Treasury of Knitting Patterns*, Schoolhouse Press, 1998.

    "   *A Second Treasury of Knitting Patterns*, Schoolhouse Press, 1998.

    "   *Charted Knitting Designs*, Schoolhouse Press, 1998.

History and Design

Falls, Dixie, *Aran From the Neck Down*, self-published, 1986. Available from the author for $16.50 ppd, 10955 Parrish Gap Road, Turner, OR 97392.

Fee, Jacqueline, *The Sweater Workshop*, Interweave Press, 1986.

Gibson-Roberts, Priscilla, *Knitting in the Old Way*, Nomad Press, 2004.

Hollingworth, Shelagh, *Traditional Aran Knitting*, St. Martin's Press, 1982.

Mysse, Janet Whitney, *The Classics: Fisherman Knits*, self-published, 1984. Out of print, but it's still possible to locate used copies.

Newton, Deborah, *Designing Knitwear*, Taunton Press, 1982.

Righetti, Maggie, *Sweater Design in Plain English*, St. Martin's Press, 1990.

Starmore, Alice, *Aran Knitting*, Interweave Press, 1997. Out of print.

Szabo, Janet, *The "I Hate to Finish Sweaters" Guide to Finishing Sweaters*, self-published, 1996.

Thompson, Gladys, *Patterns for Guernseys, Jerseys, and Arans*, Dover, 1971.

Walker, Barbara, *Knitting From The Top*, Schoolhouse Press, 1996.

Zimmermann, Elizabeth, *Knitting Without Tears*, Simon & Schuster, 1995.

Magazine Articles

"Knitting Arans From the Top Down," Beth Brown-Reinsel, *Interweave Knits*, Fall 1997.

"Alice Starmore on Aran Knitting," Jeane Hutchins, *Interweave Knits*, Fall 1997.

Knitter's Magazine, Fall 1995. An issue full of Aran-style sweaters.

"Arans, Kilt Hose, and Tartans," Elizabeth Zimmermann and Meg Swansen, *Vogue Knitting*, Fall 1995.

"Aran Sweaters," Carol Rasmussen Noble, *Knitter's Magazine*, Fall 1995. Also a
    number of Aran sweater designs included in this issue.
"Textured Knitting on Circular Needles," Marilyn Moss, *Threads Magazine*, April 1989.
"A Balancing Act: Knitter's Guide to Pattern and Proportion," Alice Korach, *Threads
    Magazine*, August/September 1989.
"Designing With Cables," Kathy Brunner with Sue M. Parker, *Threads Magazine*, October
    1988.
"Aran Knitting," Alice Starmore, *Threads Magazine*, December 1987.
"Taming the Tubular Cast-On," Parts 1 & 2, Charlotte Morris, *Knitter's Magazine*, Summer
    2001 and Fall 2001.
"Original, Textural Cables," Lily Chin, *Knitter's Magazine*, Spring 1995.
"Reversible Cables," Lily Chin, *Knitter's Magazine*, Winter 1989.
"More Reversible Cables," Lily Chin, *Knitter's Magazine*, Spring 1995.
"Advanced Reversible Cables," Lily Chin, *Knitter's Magazine*, Fall 2001.

Charting Software

Stitch and Motif Maker
by Carol Wulster, available from Patternworks
PO Box 1690
Poughkeepsie, NY 12601
1-800-438-5464
    For Windows only. A demo version is available at http://www.patternworks.com

Stitch Painter
Cochenille Design Studio
PO Box 4276
Encinitas, CA 92023-4276
Phone: 619-259-1698
e-mail: info@cochenille.com
    A demo version for either Windows or Mac is available at Cochenille's web site at
    http://www.cochenille.com

Aran Paint
Lisa Hounshell
PO Box 1002
Willagee Central LPO
Willagee WA 6156
AUSTRALIA
    A demo version of Aran Paint for Windows is available at http://opera.iinet.net.
    au/~coolhoun/index.html

Knitters Symbol Fonts
Golden Fleece Publications
824 West 10th Street
Sioux Falls, SD 57104
These fonts install directly into a word processor. They can be downloaded from http://www.knittinguniverse.com

Appendix B—
Measurements Worksheet

This worksheet provides guidance on taking body measurements, and a place to record those measurements. Make a copy of this worksheet for each of your Aran sweater projects.

Project:

Intended wearer:

Date:

Yarn used:

Needle size:

Gauge:

Measurements:

The cross-shoulder measurement is taken from shoulder to shoulder across the top of your back. Measure from the point where the shoulder drops off to the arm. In women, this measurement is usually between 15-17" (for really petite women it might be 14"). In men, this measurement is usually 18-22".

    Cross-shoulder measurement: _____

Take the full bust measurement around the fullest part of the bust or chest.

    Full bust measurement: _____

Divide this number in half to get:

    One-half the full bust measurement: _____

Add the desired ease to half the full bust measurement in order to determine the measurement to use for the width at chest:

    Width at chest: _____

In addition to those measurements, you will also need the following:

The wingspan measurement is taken from wrist to wrist across the top of the back. Arms should be bent downward (you will probably need a friend to help you with this).

Wingspan: _____

Determine the sleeve length to underarm by subtracting the width at chest measurement from the wingspan, then dividing the result in half. For example, if the wingspan is 54" and the width at chest measurement is 24", then 54-24 = 30 and 30 ÷ 2 = 15. Therefore, the sleeves would each be 15" long.

Sleeve length to underarm: _____

Measure neckline width from an existing sweater which fits the intended wearer well. Be sure to measure the full width of the opening, *not* the smaller space left after the opening is finished with ribbing or other trim.

Neckline opening without ribbing: _____

The body length to underarm can also be determined from an existing garment. Keep in mind, though, that the length of the cable patterns may affect the final length of the garment, particularly when knit from the top down.

Body length to underarm: _____

The armhole depth may be smaller than you think it needs to be. Measure an existing sweater (or several sweaters) to determine the proper fit. Alternatively, hold a knitting needle under the arm (parallel to the floor), and measure the distance from the needle to the top of the shoulder.

Armhole depth: _____

Appendix C—Key to Charts

| | Knit on RS, purl on WS

— Purl on RS, knit on WS

RT (Right Twist): On RS, K2tog without dropping sts off LH needle, then knit into the first of those two sts again

RPT (Right Purl Twist) On WS, purl second st on LH needle, then first st, then drop both from LH needle

LT (Left Twist): On RS, bring RH needle behind first st on LH needle, knit into second st on LH needle, then first st, then drop both from LH needle

LPT (Left Purl Twist): On WS, bring the right-hand needle behind the first stitch on the left-hand needle, purl into the second stitch on the left-hand needle, then the first stitch, then drop both from left-hand needle.

1/1 RC (1/1 Right Cross): Slip next st to cable needle and hold at back of work, k1, then k1 from cable needle

1/1 LC (1/1 Left Cross): Slip next st to cable needle and hold at front of work, k1, then k1 from cable needle

1/1 RPC (1/1 Right Purl Cross): Slip next st to cable needle and hold at back of work, k1, then p1 from cable needle

1/1 LPC (1/1 Left Purl Cross): Slip next st to cable needle and hold at front of work, p1, then k1 from cable needle

1/2 RC (1/2 Right Cross): Slip next 2 sts to cable needle and hold at back of work, k1, then k2 from cable needle

1/2 LC (1/2 Left Cross): Slip next st to cable needle and hold at front of work, k2, then k1 from cable needle

2/1 RC (2/1 Right Cross): Slip the next st to cable needle and hold at back of work, k2, then k1 from cable needle

2/1 LC (2/1 Left Cross): Slip next 2 sts to cable needle and hold at front of work, k1, then k2 from cable needle

2/1 RPC (2/1 Right Purl Cross): Slip the next st to cable needle and hold at back of work, k2, then p1 from cable needle

2/1 LPC (2/1 Left Purl Cross): Slip next 2 sts to cable needle and hold at front of work, p1, then k2 from cable needle

 1/3 RC (1/3 Right Cross): Slip next 3 sts to cable needle and hold at back of work, k1, k3 from cable needle

 1/3 LC (1/3 Left Cross): Slip next st to cable needle and hold at front, k3, k1 from cable needle

 2/2 RC (2/2 Right Cross): Slip next 2 sts to cable needle and hold at back of work, k2, then k2 from cable needle

 2/2 LC (2/2 Left Cross): Slip next 2 sts to cable needle and hold at front of work, k2, then k2 from cable needle

 2/2 RPC (2/2 Right Purl Cross): Slip next 2 sts to cable needle and hold at back of work, k2, then p2 from cable needle

 2/2 LPC (2/2 Left Purl Cross): Slip next 2 sts to cable needle and hold at front of work, p2, then k2 from cable needle

 1/3/1 RC (1/3/1 Right Cross): Slip next 4 sts to cable needle and hold at back of work, k1, then sl the last of the 3 sts from cable needle back to the LH needle; then (before knitting the sts) bring the cable needle to the front between needles, passing to the left of the yarn, then knit the 3 sts from the LH needle, then knit the last st from the cable needle

 2/1/2 RPC (2/1/2 Right Purl Cross): Slip next 3 sts to cable needle and hold at back of work, k2, slip last st from cable needle back to LH needle and purl it, then k2 from cable needle

 2/1/2 LPC (2/1/2 Left Purl Cross): Slip next 3 sts to cable needle and hold at front of work, k2, slip last st from cable needle back to LH needle and purl it, then k2 from cable needle

 2/2/2 RPC (2/2/2 Right Purl Cross): Slip next 4 sts to cable needle and hold at back of work. K2, slip last 2 sts from cable needle back to LH needle and purl them, then k2 from cable needle

 2/2/2 LPC (2/2/2 Left Purl Cross): Slip next 2 sts to cable needle and hold at front of work, slip next 2 (purl) sts to second cable needle and hold at back, k2, p2 from back cable needle, k2 from front cable needle

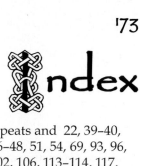

A

Aran Islands 3
Aran Knitting 3, 5–6, 25, 67,
    165–166
Aran sweaters
  definition of 5
  non-traditional 5
  traditional 5–6, 19, 36, 41,
      43–44, 54, 63, 80, 127, 131
armhole depth
  and saddles 63
Austrian Knitting 34

B

Barbara Walker 10, 13–15, 14,
    25, 33–34, 37, 52, 55, 80,
    86, 87, 110–111
Bavarian Knitting 34
bobbles 16, 21, 35, 37, 42, 69, 70

C

cabled ribbings 35. *See
    also* ribbing: within
    cables
cables
  as center panels 19–21, 26,
      29, 38, 42–44, 51, 53–54,
      58, 60, 79, 123
  common names of 15
  compatibility 46. *See
      also* design balance
  direction of 52, 127, 131
  increasing and decreasing
      into 70–71, 123
  kinds of
    braids 14, 19–22, 26, 32,
        34–35, 43, 139
    closed-ring designs 25
    diamonds 13, 21–22
    double cables 18, 26, 43
    embellished 30
    intarsia cables 10, 24, 31–32
    lace/cable combinations 23
    oddball 27
    plaits 19, 31
    ribbed cables 26, 28
    ropes 13, 16–18, 22–23,
        26–28, 43, 48
    slip-stitch cables 24, 31–32,
        36
    smocked 29
    triangles 21
    waves 17–18, 27, 28
    zig-zag 20–21, 60
  layout of 5, 40–45, 54, 81
  mirror-imaging, in designs
      119, 159
  naming of 13
  orientation 52
  using charts to represent 10,
      15, 23, 48, 51–52, 59, 170
cable needles 67
cable splay 40, 50, 51, 60, 64,
    71, 90, 91, 94–95, 99,
    103–104, 109, 115, 151
Charted Knitting Designs 165
charting software 10, 15, 59
construction methods
  body first 83
  bottom-up 21–22, 25, 35,
      50–52, 54, 59, 60, 61,
      64–65, 77–79, 89, 92, 95,
      100–101, 105, 110, 120,
      151, 157
  knit in pieces 77–78, 90, 94,
      98, 103, 109, 115, 119
  knit in the round 71, 78, 92,
      95, 101, 104–106, 110–
      112, 119, 121, 146
  neckband first 73, 80, 92, 100,
      110
  top-down 52, 73, 77, 79–80,
      83, 86, 89, 110, 120,
      131–133, 145
creativity and Aran design 6,
    39, 47
cross-shoulder measurement
    97

D

design balance
  cable compatibility and
      41–43, 45, 48
  row repeats and 22, 39–40,
      46–48, 51, 54, 69, 93, 96,
      102, 106, 113–114, 117,
      118, 121, 125–126, 127,
      129, 134, 135
  scale and 42
  vertically asymmetrical
      cables and 48
  vertical placement of cables
      51

F

Fair Isle 3
Fibonacci sequence 41, 42
filler stitches 107, 123
finishing
  edges 71
  joining saddles and body
      65, 90–92, 95, 99, 100,
      105, 128, 133. *See
      also* perpendicular join
  seaming 71, 78

G

gansey 3, 5, 7, 16, 78
garment style
  choosing a 58
  dropped-shoulder 58, 78–80,
      81, 82–88, 89–90, 93, 94,
      96, 97, 107, 108, 131–133
  peasant-sleeve 78–79, 82–83,
      85–88, 89, 97, 98, 103,
      108, 132–133, 145
  raglan sleeves 78–79, 119–
      122, 157, 160
  set-in sleeves 61–62, 63, 78,
      81, 83–84, 86, 88, 97, 107,
      108, 109, 110–115, 117–
      118, 131, 151
  T-sleeve 63, 77, 127, 128
  wide saddle 63, 131–134, 135
Garter Stitch 21, 35–37, 43, 55
gauge
  measuring 57
  row gauge 24, 36, 46, 57, 62
Golden ratio 41, 45

graph paper 10, 59, 63

I

intarsia 24, 31

K

knots, as decorative elements 37
Korach, Alice 41, 166

L

lace, in Arans 23
Lavold, Elsebeth 25

M

measurements
    armhole depth 62, 63–65, 82, 85, 87, 90, 91, 93–96, 98, 99, 102–104, 106, 108–109, 113–115, 117–118, 134, 135
    cross-shoulder 81–82, 84–85, 87, 97, 98–99, 100, 101, 103–105, 107–109, 115, 123, 131
    neck opening 81, 127, 131, 132
    of cable patterns 58
    sleeve length 127
    width at chest 78, 79, 81, 82, 84, 85, 87, 98–99, 100, 101, 103–105, 109, 115, 127, 131
    wingspan 127
mistakes, fixing 71, 72
Moss Stitch 21, 22, 36, 43–44, 51, 55, 58, 62, 146, 157–158, 166

N

neckband 73, 80, 147, 160
needles
    aluminum 10, 67
    bamboo 10
    cable needles 14–15, 27–28, 33, 67, 72, 159, 170, 171
    nickel-plated 10
    preferences 10
    wood 10

P

paired decreases 69
percentage system 119
perpendicular join 64, 90, 91, 98, 99, 109
popcorn stitches 37
projects 137

Q

quantity of yarn 9

R

Reverse Stockinette Stitch 36
ribbing
    alternatives to 60
    as trim 26, 35, 36, 47, 50–51, 59–61, 72, 73, 78, 79, 123, 139, 140, 141, 147, 158, 160
    calculating stitches for 78, 79
    within cables 26
Rice Stitch 36, 43
row repeats 46, 48

S

saddles
    choosing cable patterns for 63
    determining length of 63, 84, 133
    sewing to body pieces 65
Sand Stitch 36, 151, 152
Seed Stitch 36, 37, 43, 50, 55, 58
selvedge Stitches 71, 84
shaped front neckline 82, 86
shaping 61
    armholes 107, 123
    neck openings 40, 63, 80, 82, 83, 85, 86, 87, 89, 123, 127, 131, 132, 134, 135
    raglans 119, 120
    shoulders 108, 123
    sleeves 60, 61, 62, 63, 101, 103, 105, 108, 115
    with short rows 80, 82, 83, 108, 109, 110, 111, 115, 123
    with stepped bind-offs 108, 109, 115, 123
skirt 60

sleeves
    determining appropriate length 60
    set-in
        calculating cap shaping 61
        shallow cap 61, 109, 110, 113, 115, 117
        standard cap 27, 33, 35, 60, 62, 63, 108, 114, 115, 118
Starmore, Alice 3, 5, 25, 165, 166
stitches
    background 43, 55, 58, 59, 108, 123
    non-cabled ones, in Arans
        filler stitches 13, 16, 18, 21, 36, 38, 44, 54, 58, 59, 60, 62, 71, 89, 97, 107, 108, 123
        Left Twist 33, 34
        Right Twist 33, 34, 170
        spacers 43, 59
        stitches that twist 33, 34
        texture 33, 36, 37, 43, 89, 139
        twisted stitches 33, 34, 43, 58
stitch dictionaries 10, 23, 44, 48, 165
Stockinette Stitch 9, 24, 36, 37, 50, 58, 64, 84
swatching
    and cable layout 31, 40, 43, 44, 47, 50, 51, 57, 58, 60, 72
    for gauge 57

T

trims
    ribbing 26, 35, 36, 60, 73, 139, 140, 141, 147, 158, 160
    skirts 35, 60, 78, 79
    welts 35, 60
Trinity Stitch 10, 36, 38, 123
tubular cast-on 73, 80
twisted 21, 26, 33, 34, 35, 36, 43, 58, 64. *See also* stitches: stitches that twist

U

unshaped front neckline 82, 85

V

vests 123

W

Walker, Barbara 110
welts 60
wide saddle 63

Y

yarn
  bobbins 31, 32
  cashmere 7
  color 9, 10, 24, 30, 31, 32, 68,
      131
  construction
    plies 7, 8, 9
    semi-woolen 7
    semi-worsted 7
    woolen-spun 7, 8
    worsted-spun 7, 8
  cotton 7, 23, 67
  rayon 67
  stitch definition 8, 9
  tendency to bias 9, 27, 33
  variegated, use in Arans 32
  wool 5, 7, 23, 139, 145, 151,
      157

Z

Zimmerman, Elizabeth 58, 165